Physical Education for Melanesia

Philip J. Doecke
(coordinating author)

Kate Carpenter

Bronwyn Rakimov

S. Solomon Samuel

OXFORD
UNIVERSITY PRESS

OXFORD
UNIVERSITY PRESS

Oxford University Press is a department of the University of Oxford. It furthers the University's objective of excellence in research, scholarship, and education by publishing worldwide in

Oxford New York

Athens Auckland Bangkok Bogota Buenos Aires Calcutta Cape Town Chennai Dar es Salaam Delhi Florence Hong Kong Istanbul Karachi Kuala Lumpur Madrid Melbourne Mexico City Mumbai Nairobi Paris Port Moresby Sao Paulo Singapore Taipei Tokyo Toronto Warsaw

and associated companies in Berlin Ibadan

OXFORD is a registered trade mark of Oxford University Press in the UK and in certain other countries

First published 1999
Reprinted 2019(D)

ISBN 0 19 554123 5

Cover photograph by Ron McKie
Cover and text design by Heather Jones
Illustrations by Michael John, John Mau, Pat Kermode and Ophelia Leviny
Printed and bound in Australia by Ligare Book Printers Pty Ltd
Published by Oxford University Press
Editorial Office: PO Box 7979, Boroko NCD,
Papua New Guinea

Acknowledgments

The coordinating author would like to thank the following for their comments and assistance with the manuscript: Sam Cheung and Alita O'Keeffe from QUT; Julia Grey for her material on traditional dance.

The authors would like to thank the following students whose photographs are in this book: Alita O'Keeffe; Juliann and Dana Iselin; Melien Hopkins; Frank Perren; Leo and Susan Biggs; Linda, Dulcie, Joanne, Stephanie, Jack, and Michael Karo.

National Sports Institute of Papua New Guinea for typing first drafts of the early chapters.

The publisher would like to thank the following for their kind permission to reproduce the following photographs:
Word Publishing Co Pty Ltd PNG pp. 2, 6, 11, 25, 26, 34, 35, 71, 73, 81–4, 87, 92, 95, 96, 97, 102–3, 104–5, 108, 113, 116, 118, 121–6, 128, 135, 136–7, 138–40, 146–7, 150, 152
Philip Doecke pp. 8, 11, 26, 28, 29, 31, 36, 38, 39, 40, 45, 54, 66–7, 68, 82–3, 127, 129–30, 133, 136, 137
Alita O'Keeffe pp. 6, 8, 11, 27, 45, 73, 79.

Contents

Introduction

Physical Education is an exciting and enjoyable subject that can benefit you for the rest of your life. Physical Education means a lot more than just learning how to play a particular sport. By studying Physical Education you will also learn how your body works, how to get and stay fit, how to take care of yourself and others, and how to have some fun!

This books aims to provide Secondary students with a comprehensive range of concise and practical information that is relevant to the Physical Education course. Part One includes topics on fitness, your body, your health, sport safety and first aid, as well as recreational activities. You are encouraged to plan and implement your own fitness programmes. Part Two includes a variety of physical activities such as traditional games and dance, movement awareness, track and field, and swimming. You are invited to have a go at learning some of the skills in a safe environment. Part Three invites you to take part in some team sports that can be played by both males and females. You will learn some of the basic skills and rules needed to implement individual and group tactics to play the games. Again, you are invited to have a go and have some fun!

Throughout the book you will find the following headings and symbols. These are a signal to tell you there is something for you to do. Please make sure that you write all your answers into your own exercise book.

WORK IT OUT!

HAVE A GO!

TALK ABOUT IT!

p a r t o n e

Physical Education and You

- *Physical Education*
- *Your Body*
- *Health Care*
- *Fitness*
- *Sport Safety*

1 What is Physical Education?

Preview

Physical Education is an important subject that can help you live a healthier life. By learning about Physical Education you will be taking part in a subject that can benefit you for the rest of your life. Physical Education can help you live a healthy active life and, believe it or not, can also help you perform better in your other school subjects, or any other study that you do! You may already be doing many of the activities described in this book. This book aims to help you understand how your body can perform to its very best. With practice, and the right knowledge, you will be able to perform even better, and enjoy life to the full.

Physical activity

Physical activity has always been an important part of the Melanesian way of life. For example, people from the islands have paddled canoes over great distances and through rough seas to travel from one place to another. Women have had difficult jobs pounding tapa bark into cloth. Highlands men have had difficult work climbing steep mountains in order to hunt, or to clear the trees to build huts and fences, and use the cleared land for gardens.

All children love to run, play, explore, throw, and catch things. We all take these things for granted, and haven't thought much about them. It has been the same in other societies and cultures around the world. But in all societies and cultures, there

Figure 1.1 Traditional hunter with bow and arrows

are some physical activities that children have been taught. In Melanesian societies, the older men and women have taught the young people how to hunt, fish, garden, play games, and perform dances. And so often, small children have learnt how to perform these activities simply by watching, and then trying it out for themselves.

In our modern Melanesian society, new physical activities and skills have been introduced into the country, and they have become important to many people. We can give them the name, non-traditional activities and skills. These physical activities are played in many places around the world including at major events such as the Olympic Games, the South Pacific Games, and the World Cup tournaments. Learning about these physical activities and skills has become part of the Physical Education programme that is taught in our schools.

Figure 1.2 Modern-day sporting events

Some physical activities and sports are not played in Melanesia. Here are some examples of physical activities enjoyed in other parts of the world. Can you guess why they are not played in Melanesia?

Curling	Canada
Cross Country Skiing	Norway
Ice Hockey	Russia

Why learn Physical Education?

Here are some ideas on what Physical Education is all about.

fitness	learning how to keep the body fit and in good shape
movement	learning how to move in different situations and how to improve movement skills
health	learning how physical activity keeps the body and mind healthy
wellness	learning how the whole person works best if everything is working well together: mentally, physically, emotionally, and spiritually
sports	learning about games that are played around the world, and in Melanesia, practising the skills, and learning the rules and how to officiate the games
outdoor pursuits	learning how to enjoy physical outdoor activities, and the use and preservation of the natural environment for pleasure and enjoyment

There are many benefits and useful outcomes in taking part in a Physical Education programme. Some of these are to:

- enjoy good health
- take part in useful recreation and leisure activities
- for some, achieve excellence at their chosen sport
- recover faster after illness and injury
- enter into an enjoyable area of employment
- have fun and make new friends

One thing to note about all physical activity in school is that everyone is different. This can be in build and size, as well as in interests and skills. If smaller or younger children have to compete against children who are much bigger and stronger, the smaller children may get hurt, or may not have any success in the activity and will very quickly lose interest. For most activities children should be placed into groups of about the same age, and same build and strength. In this way every individual has a greater chance of having success in the activity and wanting to try as hard as possible. Competition should therefore be kept to a minimum in class activities. Class activities are for everybody, and nobody should be left out.

Figure 1.3 Playing together!

Recreation and leisure activities

One way everybody can be fully involved in physical activity is through leisure and recreation activities. From the beginning of time, people of all ages have taken part in recreation and leisure activities. There are many reasons why people participate in these types of activities. Recreation and leisure activities help you relax and have fun, or provide excitement and challenges. They are activities that you choose to do, other than your paid work, or the work you are obliged to do for your village or community.

If you were to conduct a survey of people in your community about why they take part in recreation and leisure activities, you would get many different answers. Here are some answers that students gave:

- to develop skills and strategies
- to keep a record of the cultural activities, heritage, beliefs and values
- to maintain health
- to keep fit
- to occupy my spare time
- to meet new people
- to feel excitement and satisfaction in having participated
- to achieve something not done before
- to try an activity from another region or country
- to relieve stress and pressures of various kinds

- to enjoy being outdoors, and experiencing the environment
- to understand myself better and more fully
- to improve my respect for others
- to work better at all my school subjects
- to develop my concentration and thinking skills
- to contribute to the welfare of my community and nation

I'm sure you can think of lots more! Recreation and leisure activities are found within your community, whether it is in the school, village or in the city. Find out about activities that have been in your community for a long time. Ask someone who knows them to teach them to you and your friends. Continue to take part in these activities after you have left school, and then share them with your friends. In this way, the activities of your community will be remembered and you will be able to appreciate, enjoy, respect and preserve your traditions and culture.

Structured and unstructured activities

The community where each of us lives has its own culture. Being physically active is important in that culture. And there are different ways in which we can be active. Some of these activities are structured. This means that there is a set pattern to be followed, which is important to the activity. This pattern may use rules and regulations. Sometimes these rules and regulations are written down, e.g. in a book of rules for playing soccer. Sometimes they are not written down, but are known and taught by the older men or women of the community. There are special occasions when they are allowed to talk about these patterns because they are important to the heritage and traditions of the community. In either situation, the activity may not be successful if the formal structure is not followed. There are many ways each one of us could participate in useful recreation and leisure activities. Here are just a few.

Structured activities

- Physical Education classes at school
- school sports
- club sports
- dances which have definite steps and movements
- gardening activities which, in order to be done properly, must use specific skills to get the desired results
- group activities

Unstructured activities

There are many activities which are physically active, which are enjoyable, yet don't need rules or regulations, or specific patterns. Here are some.

- modern dance, which tends to be an expression of movement to the rhythm and beat of the music
- hiking and walking, which may be just to follow a path, or to get a good view of the scenery, or to walk for a specific period of time
- playing with family and friends

- games of imagination
- role playing
- swimming, to keep cool

New ideas for recreation and leisure

In modern Melanesia there are new ideas which have been introduced from different parts of the world for people to use to help them get fit, keep fit and healthy, and enjoy their leisure time, e.g.

- body-building
- golf
- sailboarding
- sailing
- scuba diving
- snorkelling
- darts
- table tennis
- tae kwon do

Figure 1.4 Leisure activities in Melanesia

Some of the best recreational activities are those which don't require any cost. There are so many, e.g.

- walking
- running
- swimming
- climbing
- gardening

Then, there are those that can be done by joining a club. These clubs may charge a fee. This fee covers the costs of running the club, e.g. electricity and telephone costs, council rates for the grounds and building, building costs, mowing the field. Sometimes the club employs people such as a coach or trainer, and pays them a fee. The members usually help to run the club.

Some activities can be used to help the community in a variety of ways. There are members of the community who need help, and you, as active young people can provide this help, while keeping healthy, fit, and active at the same time. These activities might include:

- joining a young people's group in your church, e.g. Pathfinders
- joining a community youth group, e.g. Scouts and Guides
- raising funds for a charity such as the Cheshire Home
- looking after young children in the community, while adults are busy
- looking after disabled children or other people who need special assistance

Recreational activities help you learn about the world and the people around you, and help you to grow and mature so that you can contribute to your family and your community, and also feel good about yourself.

Recreation and leisure as an industry

Recreation and leisure activities are becoming important industries in many overseas countries such as Malaysia, Fiji, Australia, and New Zealand. Governments and companies are setting up facilities for people's enjoyment, relaxation, leisure, and recreation.

One way is to set aside a large area of natural, attractive land (not damaged or spoilt in any way), and allow it to be used for visitors so they can enjoy the plants, animals, birds, or views, without spoiling the land in any way. This area is called a National Park. People can hike, camp, or even have school visits to the area. They are places to relax, enjoy being together with family or friends, to walk, swim, canoe, and so on, safely, without danger. No one may set up a business or industry in the park without permission from the authorities. The only ones permitted to have a business in the area are the ones providing accommodation, food, etc. This is one example of a leisure industry.

There are other examples of businesses within the leisure industry. Communities, mining companies, hotels and resorts often provide places for members of the community to use and enjoy. Village folk can provide opportunities for visitors to see

Figure 1.5 Leisure activities in the National Parks

special places of interest. One such person is Norman Carver who lives in Goroka, in Papua New Guinea. He takes visitors from around Papua New Guinea and the world to special places in the Eastern Highlands. He has arranged these visits with the traditional landowners.

Other areas of Melanesia have beautiful beaches and reefs, and visitors enjoy exploring these places. Visitors need food and accommodation. These facilities can often cost a lot of money to run. However, they provide jobs for many people. This is an industry that can help the region become more popular for both local and overseas visitors.

The leisure industry is still very small in Melanesia. However, with the cooperation of government tourism authorities, and local landowners, it has the potential to become a very big industry in Melanesia because it is such a 'land of the unexpected'. Some students are aiming to make a career of this industry by studying for qualifications in tourism and hospitality. It is important for those who wish to be involved in such an industry to be well trained, to help people feel welcome, comfortable, and safe, so that they really enjoy their time away from home. In this way, they may wish to return to visit some more. Perhaps you might be interested in finding out more about this for your own future.

Some issues in Physical Education and sport in Melanesia

Melanesia is a dynamic and changing region of the world. The world itself is in a major state of change and development. With these changes, have come some major issues for consideration in both Physical Education and sport.

- violence in sport
- resources in schools
- resources for the community
- administration
- youth programmes
- school curriculum
- national and provincial leadership
- enthusiasm and encouragement
- positive, helpful media support from television, radio, newspapers
- elitism and professionalism

When various sports were first brought into Melanesia, problems were introduced that did not previously exist in the region. Traditionally, people have very strong relationships with those of their own language group, their own families, and with their own land. When these values are taken onto the playing-field it can be difficult to separate the sports competition from other traditional activities.

However, it's important to remember that the playing-field is not a place for violence and aggression. It is a place for cooperation, teamwork, and hard work in order to score a goal, a try, a basket, or to win a race. The most important objective is to show that you have tried your best. It is not always necessary to be a winner. In school, the most important thing is to try and improve, and become a better player. Look at this headline that appeared in a local newspaper.

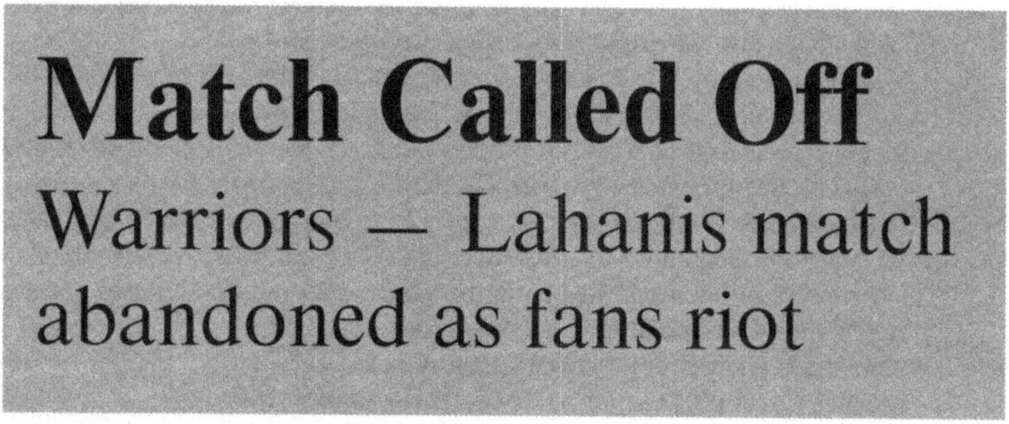

Match Called Off

Warriors — Lahanis match abandoned as fans riot

Figure 1.6 Headline in the newspaper

When a major inter-city rugby league match is being held, or a netball match between two rival teams from different areas of the country is being played, all the players should be representing their areas and their people with pride. They should be able to show that they have excellent skills and team work. Even if the final score shows that they may not have the highest score, they must know that they can feel proud, happy, and successful if they have shown excellent skills in all areas of the game.

Unfortunately some players and spectators have ideas that do not help the successful development of the sport in the country. These ideas can slow down development, and will not help the region become a really excellent sporting nation. Some inappropriate behaviour, and dangerous ideas that some people in and at sports events have are as follows:

- they believe that they are only successful if they have the winning score
- the game provides an opportunity to hurt someone from the other team
- if a team mate has been hurt, the other players feel they have to take revenge
- umpires or referees make too many mistakes
- umpires or referees come from the other team's place
- sports officials and club administrators try to make money for themselves, and don't want to improve the sport
- being a spectator gives you the right to argue with the referee, and abuse the teams from other areas

The statements written here cannot help anyone to become a better sports person. These ideas don't help anyone to become healthier and happier. They make people angry, and angry people are not good sports people. Good sports people are in control of their feelings when they get upset or frustrated. They think about what has gone wrong, and how to play more effectively. A team of well organised players, who cooperate as a team, will nearly always win over a team of stars who can't play together.

People who wish to become excellent sports people must turn all their efforts to training and practising their skills to the highest possible level. Those who use violent behaviour on the playing-field are showing that they are losers in sport because they are unable to play well, and can't control their tempers or anger. Look at some winners and champions. Of course they are excited when they win!

They are nearly always happy, friendly people, willing to help and always available to talk to someone who needs advice. They have taken on positive values of life, and show respect and concern for others. Most winners are losers before they become winners. But they don't give up and blame others when they lose. If you ask any champion they'll tell you that taking part in an event is more important than winning.

The 1996 Atlanta Olympics showed that the Melanesian representatives were able to improve on their previous performances. If they wish to proceed on to becoming international champions, then they will need to take part in carefully prepared, complex training programmes. Melanesia is still developing its facilities to be able to provide this sort of training to its sports men and women.

For every student in Melanesia, however, the main purpose of taking part in physical activity is to keep fit and healthy for the whole of life. Sports are one way of enjoying physical activity. This enjoyment should not be spoiled by those who see or use it as an opportunity to hurt someone else.

Figure 1.7 It's good to be a winner

Drugs and alcohol in sport

Another major problem associated with sports and physical activity in Melanesia and around the world, is the issue of drugs and alcohol in sport.

As soon as a game is finished, it is often considered the 'right thing to do' to go and have a drink, and to light up a smoke. There are big opposites here! Working hard for physical activity means getting your body healthy, and enjoying a long, happy life, as free as possible from disease and the effects of drugs. Alcohol is a drug, because it changes body and mental functions. Alcohol reacts badly with parts of the body that try and keep the body working properly. The body *can* deal with a little alcohol at a time. The problem is that when people drink as a member of a group, too often they can't make a good decision about when to stop.

Cigarette smoking has also been shown to cause a lot of damage to the whole body, and especially to people who want to be active and healthy. There is no positive benefit to smoking.

Figure 1.8 Quit Now!

TALK ABOUT IT!

Think about what you have learned so far in Physical Education. Have you been able to join a group that will help you take part in physical activities outside of school? Are there other students who have the same interests as you, and together you could form a club? Do you know a teacher who would help you organise a club? What activities do you already do which keep you fit and healthy? Can you name some things you do that are not helping you keep fit? Can you change these to something that would be more healthy for you?

Please note that many of the following chapters provide activities for you to do. Write your responses or answers either in your exercise book or on some paper, and not in this book.

2 Your Body

Preview

In Physical Education it is important to understand how the body is made up, and how it works. Your body is a complex machine, with different parts all working smoothly together. This chapter looks at the human body. However, it is not possible to cover all the body structures and systems here, so a selection is provided. The systems that will be looked at in this chapter are the skeletal system, the muscular system, the cardiovascular system, the respiratory system, and the digestive system. There are some activities for you to do throughout the chapter. Remember to write your answers in your exercise book or on your worksheet.

The skeleton

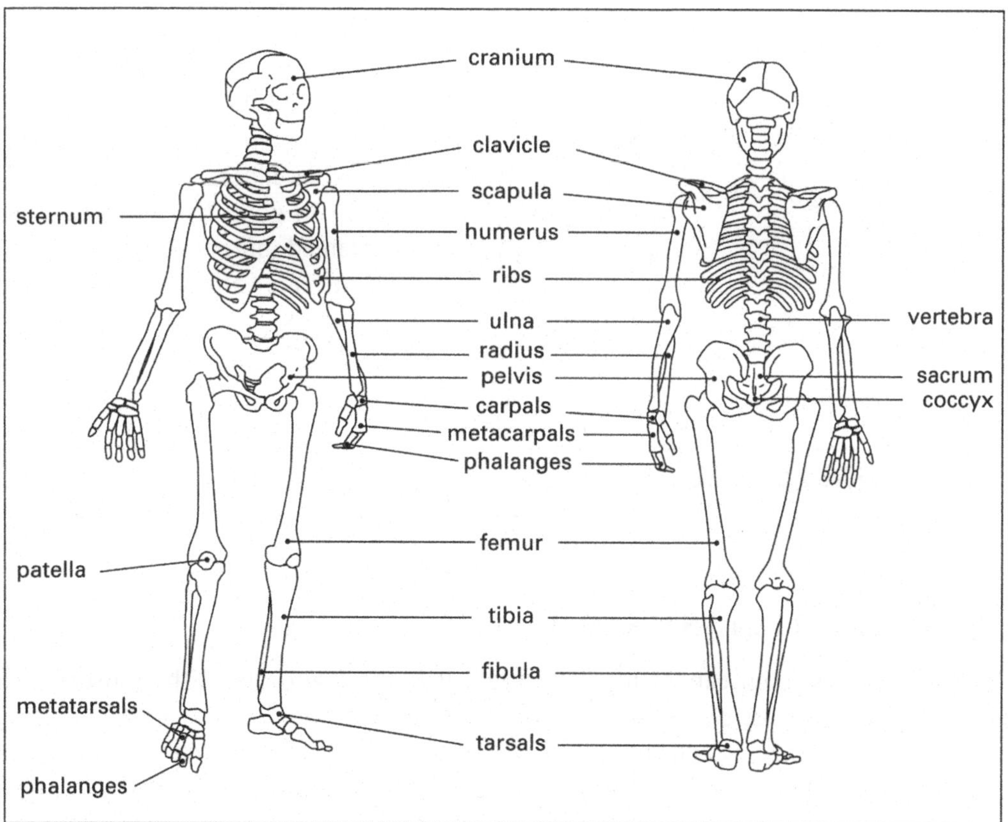

Figure 2.1 Diagram of the skeleton, front and back views

The skeleton is made up of living tissue (lots of the same type of body cells) called bone. Minerals give bone its hardness, rigidity, and most of its weight. The rest of the bone is made of protein which gives the bone its toughness and some flexibility. The main function of bone is to give the body its framework. The skeleton in Figure 2.1, is viewed from the front and back.

It is easier to look at the skeleton in several sections. If you start at the top of the skeleton and work your way down, you can look at the bones in each section. The sections may be divided up as follows:

- the skull
- the backbone, or vertebral column
- the chest
- the shoulder structure
- the arms, including the wrist and hand
- the pelvis
- the legs, including the ankle and foot

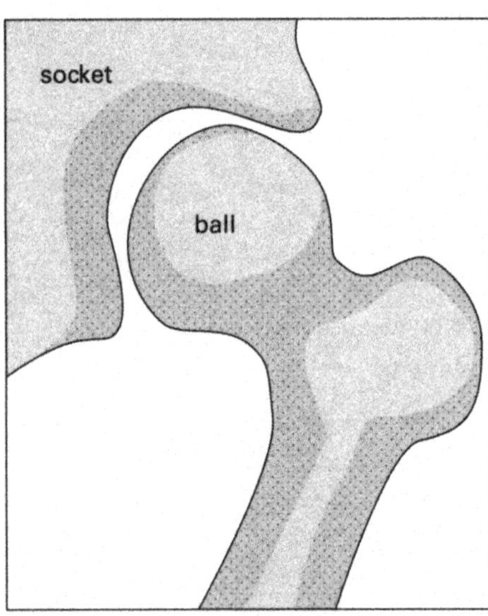

Figure 2.2 Ball and socket joint

Where two or more bones are connected and move together there is a joint, e.g. the knee joint. Some joints allow little movement, while others provide a wide range of movement. Sometimes the joints can become inflamed or swollen, resulting in an illness called *arthritis*. Another illness that affects the joints is *gout*. In gout, the joints can also become inflamed but normally only one or two joints are affected. These are painful disorders.

Muscular system

The skeleton cannot move by itself. It is the main role of the muscles to move the various parts of the skeleton. The muscles also give the body its shape. Imagine what your body would be like without muscles! The muscles produce the body's movements, support the organs, maintain posture, and produce heat. They make up about forty per cent of the body's weight, and vary greatly in size, shape, power, and function. In order to move so many complex parts, the body has three types of muscle.

1. Skeletal muscle

This is the largest group of muscles, with about 650 throughout the body. They are also the strongest. They are capable of conscious control, or acting when we want them to. Therefore they are often called *voluntary* muscles. They are filled with blood vessels and nerve endings. When you want to move a part of your body, nerve impulses (or signals) travel from the brain along outgoing nerves to the appropriate muscle.

2. Smooth muscle

This group of muscles is found in the blood vessels, the intestines and in some other internal organs. We cannot control these muscles, so they are called *involuntary*. The muscles are not very strong and so are not used for movement.

3. Cardiac muscle

This muscle is found only in the heart and requires large amounts of oxygen. Like smooth muscle, it is beyond our conscious control. It produces the strong contractions (squeezes) needed to pump blood around the body.

The following diagram shows the main muscles of the body.

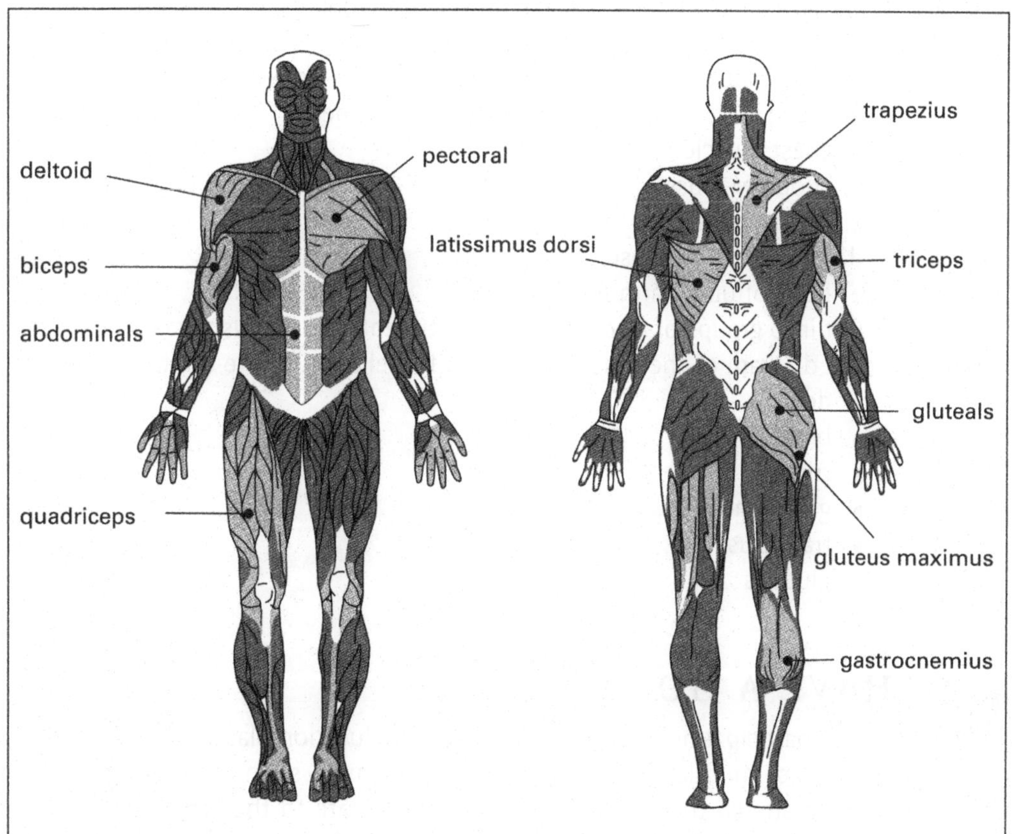

Figure 2.3 Diagram of the muscular system

Like the skeletal system it is possible to divide the body into sections in order to look at the muscles in more detail. These sections are as follows:

- head muscles
- trunk muscles (those that move the vertebral column, the chest, the abdominal muscles, and the pelvis)
- upper limb muscles (those that include shoulder movements, arm, wrist, hand, and finger movements)
- lower limb movements (those that enable leg, ankle, and foot movements)

The names of some muscles are difficult to pronounce and spell as they are from the Latin language. They are anatomical (or scientific) names. The muscles in the back of your upper leg are commonly called hamstrings, and are actually a group of three muscles that work together to bend your leg at the knee. Muscles are attached to the bone by *tendons*. *Ligaments* join bone to bone.

WORK IT OUT!

Answer the following questions, and write your answers in your exercise book. The answers to these questions will be found on page 156 at the back of the book.

1. Guess how many bones make up the skeleton.
2. Name five joints, e.g knee joint, etc.
3. Which joint do you think is the largest in the body?
4. Find the correct name of the muscles listed below.
   a. chest muscle
   b. shoulder muscle
   c. stomach muscles
   d. front of thigh muscles
   e. front of upper arm muscle
5. Get into groups of three. Select one student whose muscles can be clearly seen. Use the diagram of the muscular system to help you locate the following muscles.
   - deltoid
   - biceps
   - triceps
   - gastrocnemius
   - trapezius
   - gluteals

HAVE A GO!

When participating in sports and Physical Education classes it is important to stretch your major muscles before continuing with more strenuous activity. In your groups, select a stretch that your group can demonstrate to the class. Explain what muscles are being stretched. You do not have to use the correct anatomical name for this activity.

Cardiovascular system

The word *cardio* relates to the heart and the word *vascular* relates to the vessels that carry blood. All animals need a way of getting oxygen and food materials around the body. Every cell in the body needs oxygen and food to survive. The waste that is produced and not needed, must be removed. To deal with these needs, the body has a complex transport system. It is the blood that carries these substances around the body, in its *circulatory* system. How does this circulation take place?

The Heart

Your body has its own pump called the heart. The heart works together with the network of vessels that carry the blood. The heart is about the size of your closed fist. It lies in the chest, in between the two lungs. It has four chambers: two are called *atria* and two are called *ventricles*. The walls of the heart are made of thick cardiac muscle. The right side of the heart receives blood without oxygen (*deoxygenated*) from the body, and pumps it to the lungs. The left side of the heart receives blood with oxygen (*oxygenated*) from the lungs, and pumps it to the rest of the body. Look at this diagram of the heart.

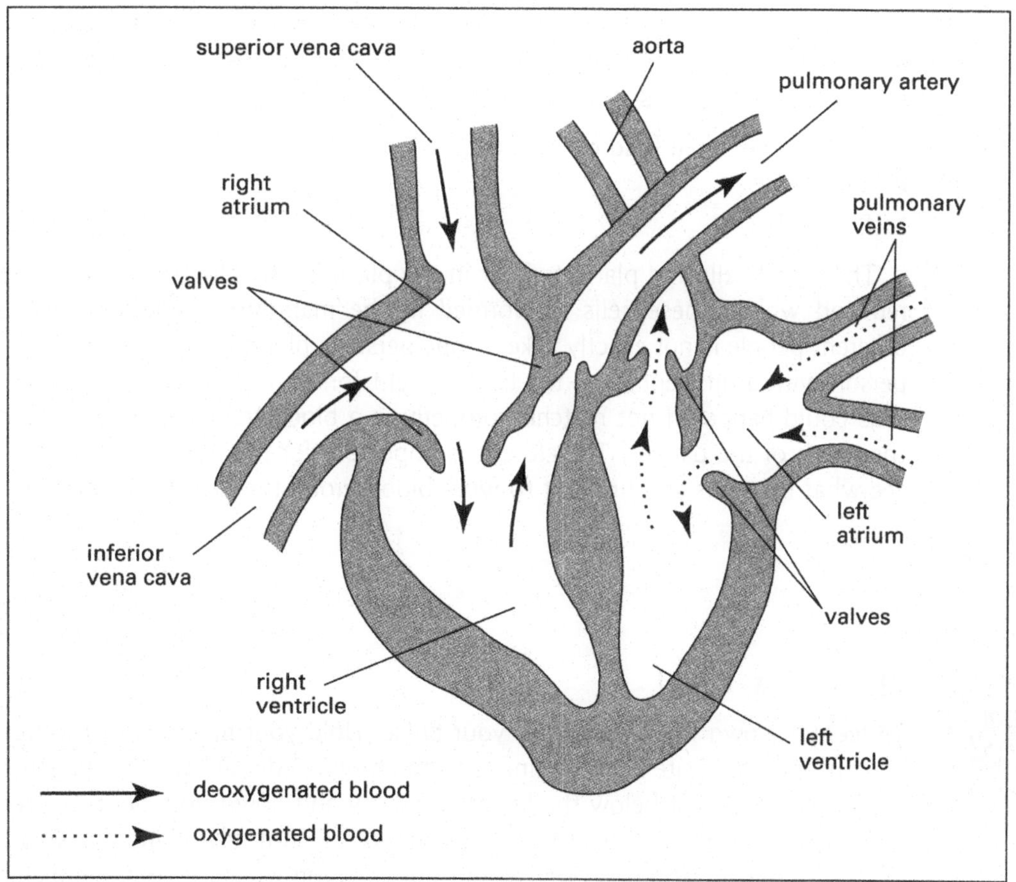

Figure 2.4 Diagram of the human heart

Even before you were born, your heart started beating when the developing embryo was about six weeks of age. From that time, in an average lifetime the heart will beat about 2500 million times. The heart's beating is caused by the contraction (squeezing) and relaxation of the heart chambers over and over again, without stopping. This repetition makes up a cycle. The cycle begins with the electrical stimulation of the heart, which is started by the heart itself. Inside the heart are valves that make sure the blood moves or flows only in one direction. The movement of the blood around the body is called the circulatory system.

The heart is the pump that sends the blood around the body. The blood has to travel in vessels or tubes. The major vessels are called the *arteries* and the *veins*. Arteries carry blood away from the heart, and the veins carry the blood toward the heart. The largest artery in the body is the *aorta*. Arteries have thick walls, but the veins have thinner walls, and the pressure of the blood against the inside of the wall is much lower.

The beat of the heart causes blood to be forced through the circulatory system. The pressure of this surge (or force of blood) is called *blood pressure*. This force is determined by the balance between the push (of the blood by the heart) and the resistance of the artery's walls. Sometimes this pressure can get too high, especially if the person is overweight, stressed, unfit, or if they have a poor diet. The pressure is so great that the heart may become strained and weakened. This person should see a doctor to receive medication and advice to improve the blood pressure so that it doesn't become a dangerous situation. The blood has three main parts:

- a yellow coloured fluid called plasma
- blood cells
- platelets

The blood cells and platelets float in the plasma. The blood cells are of two types; red and white. These cells are formed in the marrow of certain bones. Blood of different people is not exactly alike. If one person's blood is mixed with the blood of a person with a different type, the blood might form a clot (become hard like a scab). This could happen if not matched properly in a blood transfusion, and could lead to the death of the patient. Therefore it is important for the doctor to test the blood to see what type it is and find out to what blood group the person belongs.

HAVE A GO!

To feel your own heart beat, take your pulse. Hold your fingers over the front of the wrist of your opposite hand, in line with the thumb side. Or use your fingers to gently touch your neck just below the line of your jaw and down from your ear. You should feel a gentle pulsating or beating on your fingers. Count how many times you feel this beating in thirty seconds. Double your result and you will have your approximate pulse rate. Do this three times and then work out what is the average.

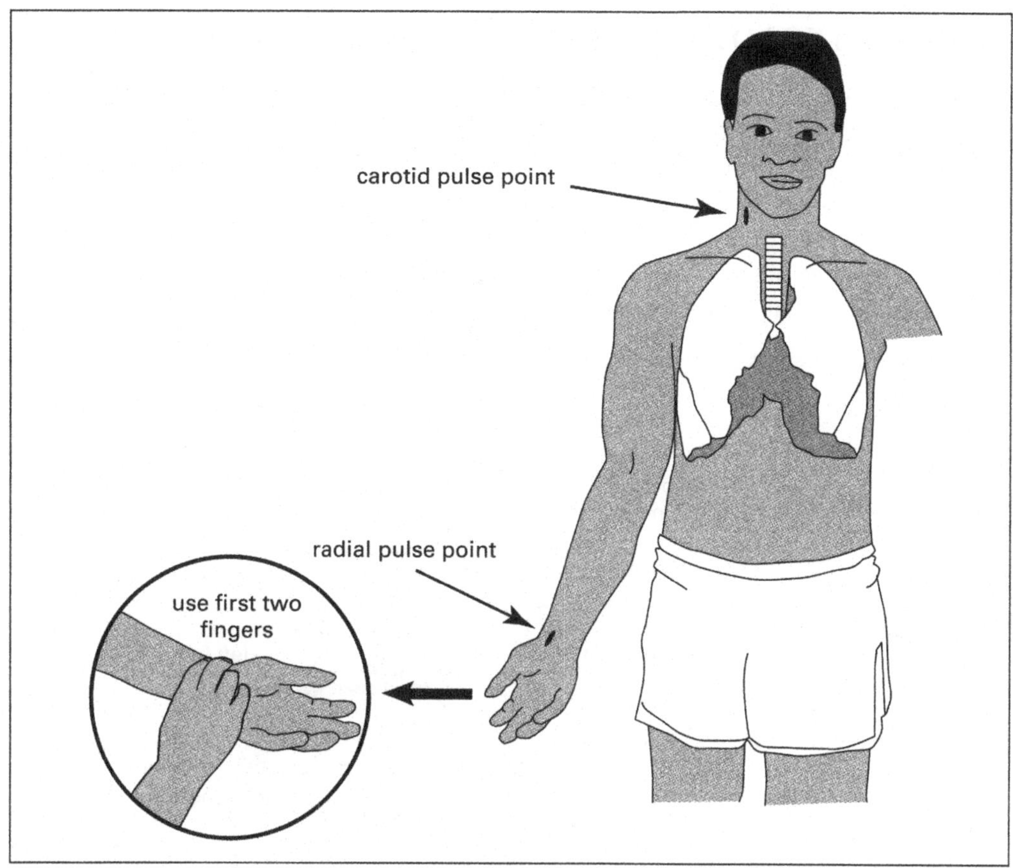

Figure 2.5 Take your pulse rate

WORK IT OUT!

Answer the following questions and write your answers in your exercise book. The answers to these questions will be found on page 156 at the back of the book.

1. The heart has four chambers (large open spaces inside). Look at the diagram of the heart and write down the name of these chambers.
2. Look at the following table. Match the statement on the left side with the correct word on the right side.

a. yellow fluid	(i) vein
b. thin walled blood vessel	(ii) pulse
c. largest artery in the body	(iii) oxygenated
d. large lower chambers of the heart	(iv) plasma
e. heart beat you can feel at your wrist	(v) aorta
f. blood with oxygen	(vi) ventricles

Respiratory system

As you are sitting and reading this book you are probably not thinking about the movement of air into and out of your lungs. You breathe in and out about ten to fifteen times per minute. Count how many breaths you take per minute. As you are counting, do you feel yourself changing your breathing pattern? It is hard not to when you are conscious of it. Respiration involves the exchange of gases in the blood, and the exchange of gases between the blood and body tissues after having breathed it in. This all occurs at various levels from the nostrils to the lungs.

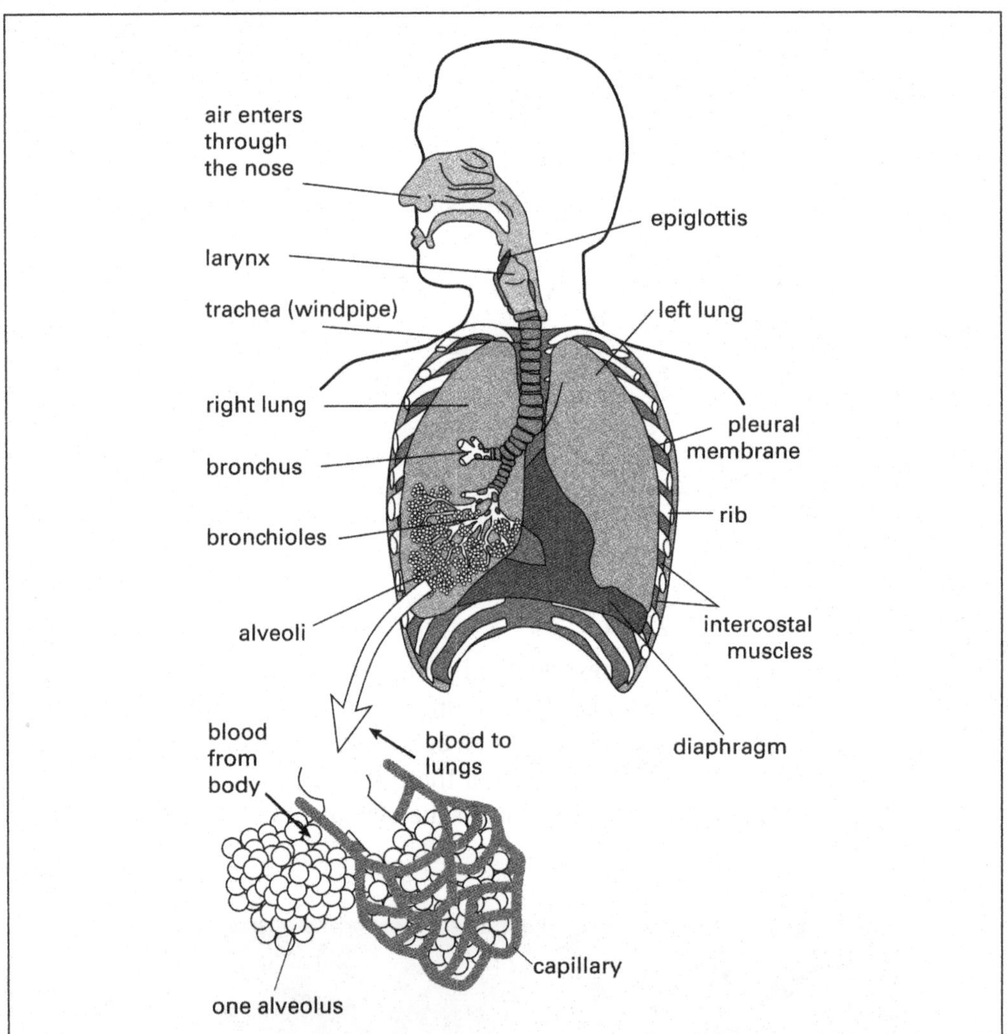

Figure 2.6 Diagram of the respiratory system

Breathing begins at the nose. Air enters through the nostrils. The hairs of your nose help to trap tiny dust particles. Membranes right inside the nose assist in warming and moistening the air. The air is filtered, warmed and moistened before it moves to its next destination, which is the *pharynx* or throat. This is where your tonsils are.

The air then moves to the windpipe or *trachea*. If you feel your own throat, you can feel ridges like rings where the windpipe is. These are rings of *cartilage*. Why do you think it is important for the trachea to have cartilage rings around it? (Other places in the body also have cartilage, like your ears, the front part of your nose, and on the ends of bone at the joint.)

In this area of your respiratory system you also have the *larynx*, or voice box. This is where your vocal cords are. At its bottom end (inside your chest) the trachea divides into two tubes. These are called *bronchi*, one of which enters each lung. Here they branch more and more, into *bronchioles*, and then into tiny air sacs called *alveoli*. There are several hundred million of these air sacs. Tiny blood vessels called capillaries surround each air sac. In the alveoli the gases of the air you have breathed in are exchanged. The oxygen from the air is absorbed into the blood in the capillaries. Carbon dioxide (used gas) from the blood is absorbed back into the alveoli, where it is exhaled to the outside air.

Your lungs are the functional organs of the respiratory system. All the other parts are mainly involved with getting the air from the outside and making sure it gets to the lungs. The lungs are soft, spongy and pyramid shaped, and are made up of several segments or pieces. They take up most of the space inside your chest. They inflate and deflate due to movements of the chest wall caused by the actions of your ribs and muscles. A sheet of muscle called the *diaphragm*, found at the base of the ribs, is especially important in making breathing take place.

During exercise the amount of air that your body needs can be up to twenty times more than when you are at rest. Your rate of breathing increases, as does the amount of air per breath. Did you know that coughing, sneezing, hiccupping, and yawning are all forms of respiration? There are different types of respiratory problems which may affect a person. Some of these are asthma, bronchitis, influenza, pneumonia, laryngitis, and emphysema. Each of these is an Acute Respiratory Infection (ARI). ARIs are a major cause of death among Melanesians. Find out as much as you can about one of these problems. Cancer may also occur in the mouth, throat and in the lungs.

WORK IT OUT!

Look at the diagram of the respiratory system. Place a piece of paper over this outline, and trace your own copy of the system. On your own copied diagram draw a dotted line to show where the air goes, starting from the nostrils. Then label the different parts of the system.

Digestive system

In order for us to stay alive, we must eat food that the body can digest. Food can be divided into several different types.

- proteins (meat, fish, eggs, cheese, milk, nuts)
- carbohydrates (potatoes, kaukau, bread, rice, bananas, cakes, biscuits, sweets)
- fats (butter, oil, ice-cream, chocolate, pork, cheese)

- fibre or roughage (bread, cereals, potatoes, bananas, carrots, cabbage, beans, nuts)
- vitamins and minerals (vitamins A, C, D, E, K, and minerals such as calcium, iron, sodium)
- water

For a healthy diet you should eat mostly vegetables, fruit, peas, beans, and cereals and only small amounts of butter, sugar, oil, and fats. If the correct foods are not eaten then the diet may be lacking in vital ingredients that keep the body functioning properly. As a result, there is a risk of developing illnesses and diseases. Examples of such illnesses are diabetes (an imbalance of body sugar and insulin) and osteoporosis (weak, brittle bones).

WORK IT OUT!

Answer the following questions and write your answers in your exercise book. The answers to these questions will be found on page 156 at the back of the book.

This section will get you thinking about what you eat.

1. On your paper make a list of the foods that you should eat the most, and decide if you are getting a good balance of the right foods.
2. You require an apple for this activity. Cut the apple into quarters so that each student in the group has one piece. Bite off and chew a piece of the apple. Discuss the following questions in your group.
   a. Which teeth are involved in biting?
   b. Which teeth are used for chewing?
   c. What changes happen to the apple while in your mouth?
3. List the letters 'a' to 'j' on your paper or exercise book. Next, read the statements and decide whether the answer is True or False. Write 'T' or 'F' for each statement.
   a. A can of Coke has over 9 teaspoons of sugar.
   b. You should not drink liquids during exercise.
   c. Bananas are fattening.
   d. We have 32 permanent teeth.
   e. Fruit juices are not fattening.
   f. Kaukau is a starchy carbohydrate.
   g. Our bodies are made up of more than 70% fluid.
   h. All people must have a diet that has all the essential nutrients in the right balance to ensure good health.
   i. Protein is essential for building and maintaining our body tissues.
   j. A high quality source of protein is fish.

Digestive tract

Were you surprised by some of the answers? Do you know what happens to the food that you eat? It has to be digested by the body. The digestive system follows a slow pathway through the body, where the useful nutrients to provide building materials

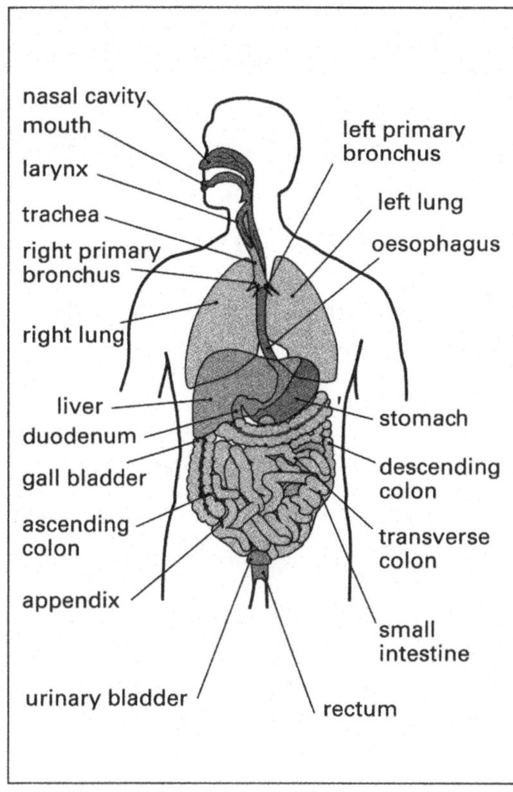

Figure 2.7 Diagram of the digestive tract

and energy for movement are absorbed. This whole pathway is called the digestive tract.

The digestive process starts at the mouth where food is torn, cut and ground into small pieces by the teeth. Saliva in the mouth helps this process, as well as the tongue and cheeks. When the food is swallowed, it passes into the *oesophagus* (or food pipe). It is moved along by strong muscular contractions to its next destination, which is the stomach.

The stomach stores the food, and continues the process of breaking down the food using gastric juices (this includes a strong acid). The food is then squeezed into the next passage, the *duodenum*, which is the first few centimetres of the small intestine. Some food such as proteins need more time to be broken down. These stay in the stomach for a longer time.

The small intestine is a narrow tube about six metres long. It is here that nutrients and water are absorbed. The wall of the intestine has many folds in it called *villi*. These folds gives the wall a very large surface area for absorption of the nutrients. There are two glands associated with this part of the system. They are the liver and the pancreas. They help provide body chemicals which digest the food. The lowest part of the digestive tract is called the large intestine. This is where water is absorbed and the body's solid wastes are produced, ready for removal.

WORK IT OUT!

Look at the diagram of the digestive system. Place a piece of paper over this outline, and trace your own copy of the system. On your own copied diagram draw a dotted line to show the pathway taken by the food into the body, and how it proceeds through the body until it is removed.

3 Basic Health Care

Preview

There are different ways of looking at the topic of health in relation to Physical Education. Health is to do with the whole person, not just whether you are sick, or have an injury. Health has to do with the different parts of your life that work together to make you a whole person. These parts include:

- physical
- mental/emotional
- social
- spiritual
- environmental

These are called the *components of health.*

Health is never the same, it is always changing. When you wake up in the morning you may experience some feelings which you are happy about, or maybe you are feeling unwell, or upset. A few hours later, at school, your feelings may have changed a whole lot more.

TALK ABOUT IT!

Spend some time thinking about the components of health. Discuss these questions in your groups.

1. Are you really healthy?
2. In which component(s) of health do you think you are strong and healthy?
3. In which components of health do you think you could be more healthy?
4. Is there some way you can improve your own health?
5. Is there someone or some people who can help you live a healthier life?
6. Are there any changes you can make that will help you live a healthier life?
7. How can you benefit if you live a healthier life?
8. How can you help those around you to live a healthier life?
9. What benefits will they experience living a healthier life?
10. Will you enjoy life more, being healthier?

Physical health

Physical health is about your body working or functioning at its best. Physical health can also be called physical fitness. Your body will function best when it is in good condition. Remember, some people may be disabled in some way, e.g. blind, or with a crippled leg, but they can still be physically in good condition.

Figure 3.1 Keeping in good condition

A person is physically healthy when s/he:

- gets enough exercise
- has strength, flexibility, and endurance
- has speed, power, balance, agility, coordination, and quick reactions,
- resists infections and communicable diseases
- eats correctly
- gets enough rest and sleep
- has an ideal weight for his/her body height, age, and sex

However, lots of things can prevent the body from working at its best, e.g. injury, sickness, poor food, not enough food, too much of the wrong kind of food, old age. Many people are in good health as children and teenagers, but get sick as they get older. The types of food eaten, and doing less exercise also contribute to reduced health. When a person's health is poor, the body is unable to protect itself from disease. It takes much longer for the immune system in the body to fight the disease, and for the person to recover. When injured, the body takes a longer time to heal. In the towns, people are doing less exercise. They don't spend as much time working in the gardens, going fishing, cutting kunai grass, and so on.

Research and studies carried out by doctors and health scientists have shown that our bodies need a variety of foods, more of some, and less of others. In Melanesia, many people in villages and towns eat only one or two types of food. Their bodies don't have stores of necessary vitamins and minerals. When people do get ill or injured, medical help is often far away, and the medical centre may not have enough of the right kind of medicine for the nurse or doctor to give to the sick person.

Overall, people could do quite a lot to improve their own health. A healthy lifestyle could enable people to live longer lives, as well as improving the quality of their life. For many reasons, most Melanesians don't live as long as people in other countries. By thinking carefully about life in Melanesia, and carefully planning for improved use of available resources, much can be done to help everyone to live more healthy lives. Planning, sharing, and preventing waste of resources will do much to assist.

Mental/emotional health

A person is in good mental health when s/he enjoys thinking about things, planning activities for the future, and solving problems without getting upset. This is why mental health is also known as 'emotional' health. The way you feel inside, is also shown to those around you, by the way you talk and the way you behave.

Figure 3.2 How do you think the people in the photographs are feeling?

Sometimes your emotions are shown automatically, without you having to think about it. This is usually the case with babies and children. As we get older, we often choose to hide or control our emotions. The way we really feel is not always seen or noticed by someone else. Sometimes we hide our feelings to protect ourselves, or to keep a secret. Sometimes we do it because we don't want other people to know how we feel.

The mind and the emotions can be complex and difficult to understand. They are different from one person to the next. They are however, an important part of who we are and why we sometimes do what we do. When we are in control of our mind and our emotions, we feel comfortable with ourselves, and we behave in ways that are acceptable to those around us. We are mentally (and emotionally) healthy.

Sometimes people like to eat, drink, or take substances into their bodies because it changes their feelings in ways that they like. Examples of these substances are wine and beer, which contain alcohol; cigarettes, which contain nicotine; and betel nut, which is a mild depressant drug. A decision that the user must take when choosing to use these substances is to understand the changes that these substances make to the mind and body. These changes are shown through our emotional and mental behaviour. For the user, these changes often feel good. Very often, however, these changes in mood and behaviour are not at all helpful or pleasant. Too much of the substance at one time, and if used for too long, can have poisonous or other long lasting effects on the body. The mind can also have long lasting changes made because of this substance.

Figure 3.3 Pick the winners and losers in this photograph

Social health

Do you get on well with everyone? Do you enjoy being with people? Are people happy to be with you? People are important to our daily well-being. These people may be your family, your friends, your wantoks, the other people in the village or town, and the people you go to school with.

Most people enjoy being with other people. Melanesians love being with their families and their wantoks. It is important for the family and clan, to keep friendships, to offer support, and help each other plan activities and make decisions. Even in the towns, members of families and language groups enjoy being with each other. Someone travelling to town usually visits wantoks and often stays with them. Increasingly, they also learn to enjoy meeting people from other parts of the country and from overseas countries.

When you are with someone who you know well, you feel good and comfortable. If you have an argument or disagreement, it is often easier to work out an answer with someone you know. Being 'socially healthy' therefore means to be able to live with and around other people, and be able to cooperate and share things with them. Social health has to do with ways of acting and behaving. It describes the level of satisfaction that an individual gets from being with other people.

Figure 3.4 Having fun with others

When you have a job to do, or duty and responsibility to perform, this is also a social activity. It is social because it has to do with people. It's not always easy to have good relationships, however. There are some people you will always feel uncomfortable talking to, or even being near. For your sake, and also for the other person, it is often best not be near them until you are able to talk with them without feeling bad, or angry, or ashamed.

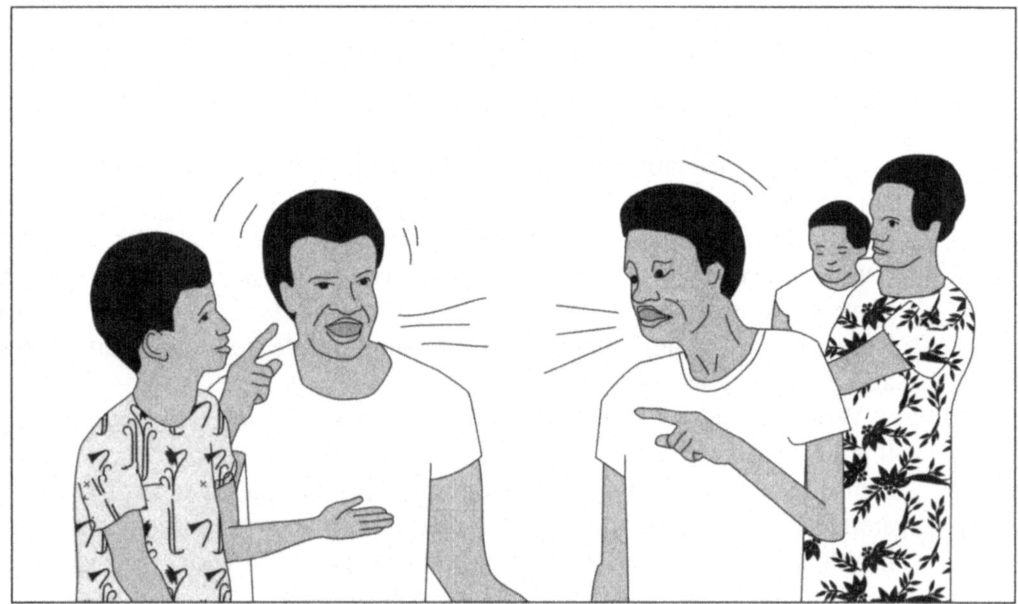

Figure 3.5 Is this the right way to solve a conflict?

Spiritual health

Spiritual health is that component which considers the ideals, purposes, and goals for life. It considers relationships, the quality of the relationship, and the love and care shown by someone towards someone else. It is shown through an appreciation of beauty, an expression and application of creativity, and a desire to understand higher order issues such as an awareness of the purpose of life, and how this contributes to a better society for others and oneself. This might be expressed through a religious faith, which is a central part of the Melanesian way of life, and determined in the opening statements of the Constitution. It is practised by most people across the nation as being a important part of the individual's and national development.

Spiritual health is important to all people, and everyone has some way of being spiritual. Some people show it through focusing all their efforts and energy inwards, inside themselves. Those who are spiritually healthy have a peace, calmness, and joy of life about their personality. This is shown through their love and respect in their behaviour towards others.

Figure 3.6 A church youth group

Environmental health

In the past few years, people in Melanesia have become more concerned about environmental health. This refers to the quality and maintenance of the environment. The environment means all the things around us. This might be natural things such as the trees, the bush, the mountains, the beach, the sea, the rivers. It might also be man-made things such as roads, houses, mines, and factories.

Most of our people still live in villages. There is a lot that can be done to make sure that the environment is safe and healthy for everyone who lives there. For it to be successful, everyone in the community needs to cooperate so that the whole community will benefit. Here are some things that will contribute to safety and improved health around the village. They have been suggested by Physical Education students at the National Sports Institute.

The village

- Keep pathways clear of rubbish, rocks, glass, and other dangerous objects.
- Don't have paths and houses under coconut palms. Falling coconuts can be dangerous.
- Put up fences near cliffs, riverbanks, steep slopes, or other dangerous places to prevent young children from falling, or to protect anyone walking at night.
- Dig deep pits and trenches to deposit the rubbish, then cover with a lot of soil when nearly full. Keep these pits well away from houses, and fenced off from children or pigs. Do not leave metal, bits of broken wood, or glass lying around. Wrap broken glass up before burying it deeply.

The house

- When getting rid of rubbish from the house, bury scraps and other things that can rot into deep pits. Get information from health centres and agriculture offices to show how food scraps may be recycled (used again, or converted) for mulch or compost to improve the soil in the garden.
- Unwanted paper and cardboard can be carefully burned, away from the village. Again there are methods for soaking old paper and cardboard until it is really very wet, then squeezing the water out of it until dry, and using it for building blocks or firewood.
- Be very careful with attempting to burn most plastics, and some rubber. The smoke can be poisonous and make you sick. Never try to burn tins and cans. Old car or truck tyres can be filled with soil, then used to hold slopes and banks against rain washing them away.
- Use proper bush toilets with deeply dug pits, covered and protected from insects. Always cover them when not in use. Make sure the contents cannot drain into rivers, streams, or lakes that might be used for washing and drinking. Government and church community health centres can provide information on how to build toilets properly and safely. Try not to use the bush, rivers, or streams as toilets.
- Help your family choose the right place to build the house. Watch for where water will flow during heavy rain. Does the water flow away from the house? Could the ground move under or near the house? Is it solid?
- Help your parents keep the house in good condition. Replace any broken posts or rails, beams, or other wood, or cover any holes that could hurt someone. Keep the roof in good condition against the rain.
- Never light a fire inside a house that does not have fresh clean air passing through it. Breathing a lot of smoke, especially sleeping inside a very smoky room, can cause a lot of illness.

Ourselves

- Make sure the water you drink is always fresh, clean, and pure. When you have a good supply, drink plenty of it but do not waste it.
- Check chapter 5 for details concerning keeping cuts and other injuries clean so they will not become infected.

- Check chapter 9 for safety and health concerning swimming.
- Wash regularly, and then dry yourself properly. Diseases can grow in moist parts of your body, such as under your arms or between your legs. You will know if you have an infection if these parts become itchy, uncomfortable, and sore. If they become uncomfortable, there are suitable medicines available which can help clear up the infection. If it gets worse then you will need to see a doctor, nurse or medical orderly.
- Any breathing illness may cause you to sneeze or cough, or have a runny nose. Be very careful of any fluid you sneeze out or cough up. Each time you sneeze or cough, you force out millions of invisible, tiny drops of moisture-carrying disease particles. But these particles carry enough disease for those near you to breathe in, and to catch your sickness. Carry and use tissues, and throw them into a rubbish bin when finished. If you use a clean handkerchief, wash it thoroughly when finished. Try never to spit or cough onto the ground where others will walk or sit. If you have to cough or spit, and you don't have a tissue or handkerchief, make sure it is right away from where it will interfere with anyone else.

Health and disease

Acute Respiratory Infections (ARI) are some of the biggest killers in Melanesia. These diseases include pneumonia, influenza, and bronchitis. They may start from simple coughs and colds, or runny noses, but are highly contagious (very easily passed on from one person to another). Malnutrition, diarrhoea, and malaria make children more vulnerable to ARIs. Clean air is also essential for avoiding the disease. Good health and hygiene practices, as discussed in the previous paragraph, are very important for everyone to use.

Figure 3.7 Don't spread germs

Diseases that are transmitted by having sex are called Sexually Transmitted Diseases (STDs) and are becoming more of a threat to the health of the community. The types of diseases range from annoying sores like genital herpes, to the deadly HIV (Human Immunodeficiency Virus) and AIDS (Acquired Immune Deficiency Syndrome) virus that is killing millions of people around the world. These viruses are carried in human fluids such as blood, semen, and saliva.

People make choices about whom they have sex with. Nowadays, many young people are putting themselves and others at risk by choosing to have sex with more than one partner. One infected person having sex with several other partners can spread the disease quickly. Anyone having sex with more than one partner should protect themselves from contact with blood or semen from the other person. Condoms are available from various suppliers, including chemists and health centres. However, condoms are not totally reliable because they depend on the user fitting the condom correctly. More information can be obtained through doctors and community health centres. Where people choose to commit themselves to one lifelong partner, the risk of getting an STD is very greatly reduced.

Possibly the biggest problem with diseases such as AIDS and HIV is that (at the time of writing) there is no cure; neither is there likely to be a cure for many years yet. Anyone who gets AIDS has AIDS for life. Sometimes it may not appear to affect the person at all, and they may not know that they have the virus. The person may have sex and, without knowing it, infect their partner(s). But most often, the person's immunity (natural defences against diseases and illness) will fail, and the person may die from any number of simple illnesses. Even a common cold or malaria will kill the person very quickly.

WORK IT OUT!

Answer the following questions and write your answers in your exercise book. Discuss your answers with the rest of the class.

1. Health may be divided into several components. These are . . .
2. List anything around your community that could be dangerous to your community's environment, and therefore to the health of the members of the community.
3. In groups, or as a whole class, plan ways of improving areas of the environment so that they are no longer dangerous. What other benefits may be found because of the changes your group is planning?
4. List some changes that could be made in your home, your school, or your community, to reduce the risk of disease.
5. Once you have made some decisions about how to improve the health of the community, carefully plan how you would go about informing others, to ensure that they also see these changes as being important.

4 Your Fitness

Preview

Physical fitness means being able to carry out everyday tasks without feeling too tired, and to have enough energy to enjoy sports and recreational activities. To be physically fit you must exercise regularly.

The level of physical fitness depends on your daily lifestyle. If you are a very active person your level of fitness will need to be higher than those who are not so active. Generally, as you get older physical fitness declines due to ageing and being less active. You can keep yourself physically fit in a variety of ways.

The traditional village lifestyle of cooking, gardening, fishing, building houses, hunting, and walking still remains in Melanesia. This is a lifestyle that is physically demanding and requires a high level of fitness to cope with day-to-day living. However, in urban centres, physical activity is decreasing because of the increase of modern lifestyles. In urban centres, the traditional active way of life is being replaced by office jobs, watching television, playing computer games, driving cars, and using electrical home appliances. There is now a need to balance the convenience of a modern lifestyle with physical activity to remain fit and healthy.

The importance of physical fitness

Performing physical exercise and becoming physically fit is important for a number of reasons. It helps to develop and maintain good health by:

- reducing the risk of diseases such as heart disease, respiratory diseases, obesity, cancer, and diabetes that may have been caused by the way we live
- maintaining a healthy weight range
- improving body functions and performance

It gives us a positive feeling of well-being by:

- promoting high self-esteem and confidence
- making us feel good about ourselves and the way other people see us.

It develops an attitude of being 'fit for life' by:

- making regular exercise and sport an important part of our lifestyle
- making us want to keep fit and healthy

It enables us to cope with a daily lifestyle that includes activities such as gardening, working on a building site, taking part in school activities, playing sport, looking after a family, etc.

Types of physical fitness

If physical fitness is 'the ability to carry out everyday activity without becoming too tired', what types of physical fitness are necessary to do this?

There are many areas of fitness that contribute to being in good physical condition. The importance of each area of fitness will depend on the reason you want to be fit. It may be to play a chosen sport, to perform better at home, school or work, or it may be for health reasons. For example, power walking is popular for the health conscious person wanting to develop cardiovascular endurance; a labourer needs good muscular strength and endurance, but doesn't need the flexibility that a dancer requires. Each area of fitness requires a different form of exercise. Weight and resistance training will increase strength but will not develop flexibility. In the same way stretching will improve flexibility but will not change the structure of your body. Knowing what is the purpose of your exercise and what you are trying to improve is just one of the principles of training. Here are the five main health-related fitness components.

1. Cardiovascular endurance

Cardiovascular endurance is considered to be the most important type of fitness essential for good health. Its main feature is non-stop exercise which improves the ability of the heart and lungs to deliver oxygen to the working muscles, and remove carbon dioxide and waste. Cardiovascular endurance is also known as heart-lung fitness, stamina, or aerobic fitness. Ways to improve endurance are through taking up jogging, walking, bush walking, swimming, paddling a canoe, cycling, or attending aerobic classes at a fitness centre.

Figure 4.1 Jogging and swimming are good ways of keeping fit

2. Muscular strength

The maximum weight an individual can lift is known as muscular strength. Strength training using weights like those found in a fitness centre or gymnasium, makes muscles bigger. This means you are able to lift heavier weights or, in scientific terms, exert a greater force. Strength can also be improved by resistance training. The easiest form of resistance that doesn't require any expensive equipment is using your own body. Exercises such as push-ups and sit-ups develop muscular strength. Strength is important when kicking a soccer ball a long way, throwing a softball, and in everyday activities such as carrying young children, firewood, or heavy rice bags.

Figure 4.2 Weight training

3. Muscular endurance

Have you ever sat a school exam or test and had sore fingers from writing so fast and answering many questions? This is an example of a type of fitness known as muscular fitness. It is the ability of a muscle to keep working for a long time. Holding a pen, having an upright posture, or performing a number of sit-ups, are all examples of muscular endurance.

Figure 4.3 Circuit training develops muscular endurance, as well as improving cardiovascular endurance and muscular strength

4. Flexibility

Flexibility means the range of motion or movement around a joint in the skeleton. Some joints are more flexible than others because of the way the joint is constructed. The shoulder joint has a larger range of motion than the elbow joint. The shoulder joint is known as a ball and socket joint. It allows the joint to rotate. The elbow joint is known as a hinge joint and is only able to bend in one direction. Try it out for yourself!

Muscles also limit flexibility, but regular stretching can improve this. The muscle can be thought of as an elastic band. A gradual stretch held for about 10–15 seconds will lengthen the muscle slowly. A sharp short stretch may snap the elastic band, and in the body cause injury to the muscle. Dancers, gymnasts, athletes, and swimmers all need good flexibility.

Figure 4.4 Stretching to increase flexibility

5. Body composition

Body composition describes the way your body is made up. It depends on how much fat and muscle you have for your height and weight. It is important for health and your performance in the sporting arena that you have an acceptable body composition depending on your age, sex, height, and body shape or type. The simplest way to tell if you have the ideal body composition is by weighing yourself and comparing this to a height/weight table. One problem with this method is that while you might be 'overweight' you may not be over-fat because your body could be very muscular, like many Highlands people.

Another method to describe body type is to take a 'pinch test' or 'fat test'. This test measures the amount of fat that is located just beneath the skin. How much skin can you pinch together with your fingers? Measurements are taken at different sites on your body, for example, your biceps, triceps, abdomen, hip, and shoulder blade area. These are then compared to body fat tables to give a total percentage body fat reading.

Females generally have a higher acceptable reading than males due to female hormones. Fatty deposits are usually located around the thighs, hips, and buttocks in women, and around the abdomen and chest in men. The fatty deposits are more dangerous to men's health because they cover vital organs such as the heart and lungs. Being obese (or overweight) makes your body work overtime and places an extra strain on your heart, lungs, and joints. When you play sport and games you tire easily, which is another disadvantage of being overweight.

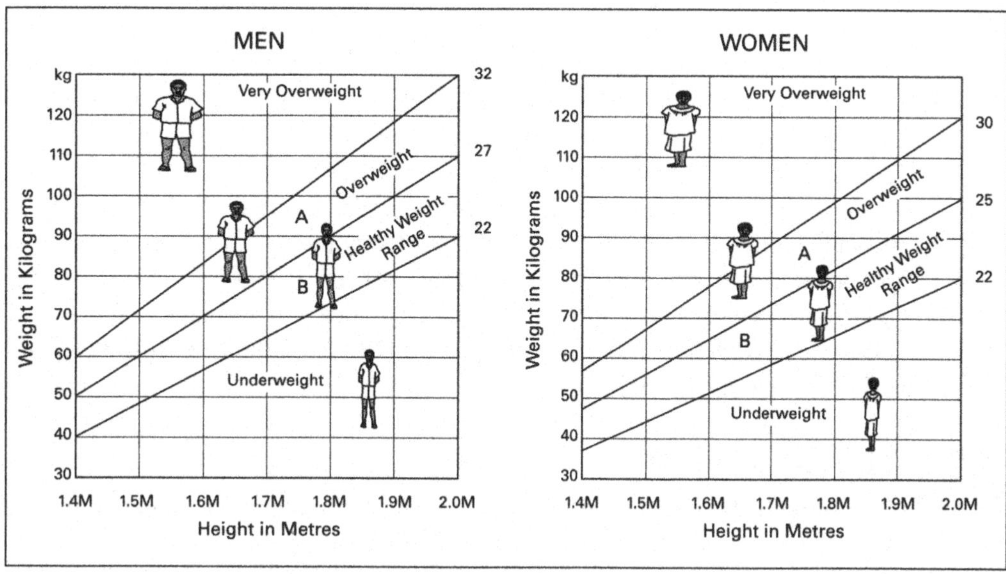

Figure 4.5 Height and weight charts for men and women

WORK IT OUT!

1. Work with a partner. Look at the height and weight charts (one is for males, and the other is for females). Measure and record your partner's height and weight. Look at the chart. How does your result compare to what is noted on the chart? Are you in the healthy range?
2. The six skill-related fitness types are **power**, **speed**, **agility**, **balance**, **reaction time**, and **coordination**. They are important parts of all sports but are not necessary when developing fitness for health. Name the different health-related fitness components shown in the following pictures.

Figure 4.6 Different ways of keeping fit

Measuring physical fitness

How fit are you? You probably have some idea of what physical condition you are in. If you are out of breath climbing a short flight of stairs or running to catch a PMV, your fitness level is likely to be poor. Your true state of physical fitness can be assessed by correctly doing a fitness test. There are two different types that are usually chosen. The first measures your general state of health and might be used in a Physical Education class. The second is a test designed for sports teams and includes components of fitness necessary for that particular sport. For example, a fitness test for volleyball might include a vertical jump test. The results of the test will rate your current fitness and give you a starting point for your exercise programme.

Field testing is the most popular form of fitness testing in Melanesia. This is because it is inexpensive, simple to organise, easy to monitor, and is very reliable. More than one person can be tested at once, which means a field test is ideal for the school situation. Usually the only equipment that is needed is a large playing field and the people involved. The other type of testing is called laboratory testing which requires expensive, sophisticated equipment.

HAVE A GO!

Try doing the Four-Factor Fitness Test. It can be completed in an eighty minute Physical Education session. All the necessary information on how to run the four tests, the results, and the rankings can be found in the book, *Physical Education Trial Assessment Guide : Grades 7—10* (published by the Papua New Guinea Department of Education, 1985). Your teacher will help to carry out the tests.

1. The 12 minute run test

This test measures endurance (or stamina). You must complete as many laps as possible of a 400 metre track (or the playing field) in 12 minutes. The more laps completed, the greater your stamina.

Figure 4.7 Students doing the 12 minute run test

2. Sit-up test

The sit-up test measures your muscular endurance and tests how long and how fast your abdominal muscles can work before becoming exhausted. The more sit-ups you perform, the better your muscular endurance fitness is. Girls have one minute to perform the test while boys have two minutes.

Figure 4.8 Sit-ups

3. Sit and reach test

This is a flexibility test which measures how far your hamstrings (muscles in the back of the legs) can stretch. Girls generally have better flexibility than boys because of hormonal differences. Practise this test in pairs.

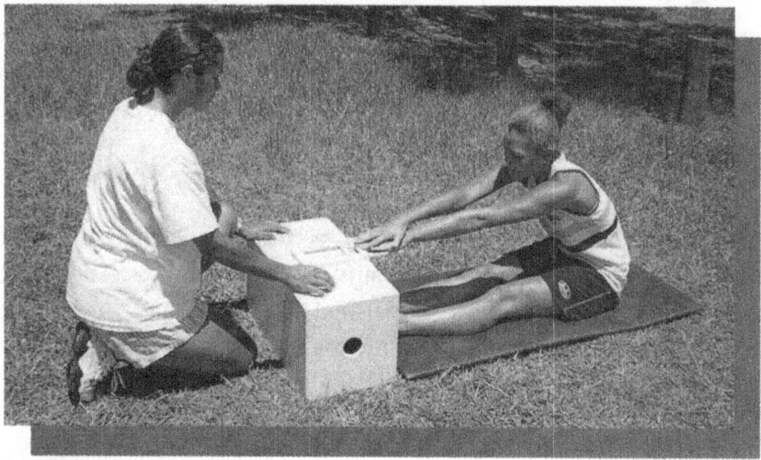

Figure 4.9 Sit and reach

4. Flexed arm hang

This test measures the fitness component of strength. Students must support their own body weight and hang for as long as possible from a bar above the ground. Staying in this position for a long time means you have good upper body strength. See for how long you can hold this position.

Figure 4.10 Flexed-arm hang

Designing a fitness programme—F.I.T.T.

A useful way of keeping fit is to design a fitness programme for yourself. In this way you can use activities that interest you. The F.I.T.T. principle covers the four essential areas required to design an exercise programme. These areas are frequency, intensity, time, and type.

F = Frequency

This means the number of workouts or training sessions performed each week. Fitness can't be stored, but it can be developed and maintained. Exercising once a week provides little improvement in fitness. Exercising three times per week is a minimum. Although exercising on concurrent (one after the other) or alternative (every second) days provides the same fitness benefits, alternative days prevent fatigue, injury and maintain motivation to continue your programme when first starting out.

I = Intensity

Intensity means the level of exertion or how physically demanding the activity is. Walking to school would be classified as low-intensity exercise whereas completing a number of 100 m sprints would be a high-intensity activity. Heart rate is a good way to show how intense the exercise is or how hard your body is working. As the intensity of the activity increases, your heart and breathing rate increases in order to match the increased work load of the muscles.

Heart rate can be measured by taking your pulse at either the radial artery in the wrist or the carotid artery in the neck (see Figure 2.5 on page 19). The pulse rate is also used to find a *Target Training Heart Rate (TTHR)* which tells you how hard or at what intensity to exercise. A range or zone is helpful so that you exercise at a rate that is high enough to achieve a training effect, yet low enough to allow you to exercise for the right length of time. For cardiovascular endurance fitness you should aim at exercising between 70%–85% of your maximum heart rate (that is, the fastest your heart can pump). For more intensive exercise, known as anaerobic training, your TTHR will be even higher: at 85–100%. A formula has been developed to work out your Target Training Heart Rate.

200 – age = Maximum Heart Rate (MHR)
MHR x intended training intensity = TTHR beats/minute.

For example, the TTHR calculation for Kila, a 15 year old girl, would be as follows:
200 - 15 = 185 (MHR)
185 x 0.70 = 128 beats/minute
185 x 0.85 = 157 beats/minute

The target training heart rate zone for Kila would therefore be between 128 and 157 beats per minute. A simple rule to remember is that when doing cardiovascular exercise you should be able to continue talking while exercising, otherwise it is too intense.

T = Time
Research has shown that twenty minutes of continuous exercise is needed to develop cardiovascular fitness.

T = Type
You should choose a type of exercise to suit the component of fitness that you want to develop. It is very important to choose an activity that you enjoy. You are more likely to stick to your exercise programme if you choose your favourite sport or exercise. So if you don't like wearing a bathing costume perhaps swimming should not be included in your training programme!

Fitness can't be stored, so the benefits maintained from exercising will only remain if you keep at it. To increase your fitness level you must 'overload the system' and increase the work done by your body by increasing any of the F.I.T.T. factors. Remember, start slowly and build up gradually. Don't rush straight into tiring, painful exercise. You won't want to continue for very long.

HAVE A GO!

1. Work out your TTHR zone for endurance fitness activities. That is, 70%–85% of your MHR.
2. Take your resting pulse at the wrist or neck for one minute. Record this.
3. Now jog continuously around a large field for five minutes, stop and take your pulse for one minute. Record this.

4. Explain why your exercising pulse is greater than your resting pulse.
5. While jogging were you in the TTHR zone?

A training session

Each time you exercise there should be three separate parts of the session. These are the warm-up, the conditioning phase, and the warm-down.

Warm-up

The purpose of the warm-up is to prepare the body for the exercise activity which is to follow. This will prevent (or at least reduce) muscle injury and soreness. The warm-up should raise the body temperature and increase both the heart rate and the breathing rate.

There are two parts to the warm-up: a continuous aerobic activity such as slow jogging, followed by the second part, stretching. The aerobic part of the warm-up should continue long enough for the individual to start sweating and puffing. This means the muscles are now warm enough to be stretched.

Conditioning phase

The conditioning phase develops the specific fitness component using chosen training methods. If strength is to be developed the conditioning phase might include partner activities with weights, or personal strength building exercises. Where suitable facilities are available, these could include weight training and weights circuit classes. Intensity, frequency and type of exercise are all important parts of the conditioning phase.

Warm-down

The warm-down may also be called the 'cool-down'. It does just that: cools the body down after exercising by reducing the heart rate to 100–120 beats per minute. The cool-down should be a continuation of the conditioning activity but at a very reduced intensity, for example, from running to walking. Stretching completes the cool-down.

5 Sport Safety and First Aid

Preview

Injuries and sickness can happen to anyone at any time and any place. This chapter will discuss what may happen, why it happens, and what you can do if something happens to you or your friends while playing sport, or while just being physically active. Sometimes a teacher or adult may not be around to help. Sometimes, even if they are, they may not be able to help.

The ideas and activities listed here can't help in every situation. But they can help you decide what to do if an accident or injury occurs at school or when playing games or other recreational activities. First aid can best be learned by doing a special course, run by a doctor, qualified nurse, or ambulance instructor. Your teacher may also be able to teach you if he or she has done an instructor's course in first aid.

Prevention

Prevention is the best way to avoid an accident or injury. However, being physically active encourages taking risks, and often taking these risks is an important part of the success of the activity. Every effort should be made to reduce the chance of anyone getting hurt. Here are some of the best ways of preventing an injury.

- keep yourself fit
- don't play if you are ill, e.g. if you have malaria, diarrhoea, or the flu
- don't play if you have an injury which has not completely healed, e.g. sprained or strained muscle
- cover any sores or cuts
- ease up or stop the activity if you get hurt or feel any pain
- be well rested
- be well nourished, e.g. have proper food and water
- if recently ill or injured, return to the activity slowly and progressively
- warm-up and stretch carefully before heavy activity
- choose activities for which you are best suited
- wear suitable clothing for that activity
- keep any necessary equipment, e.g. boots or sneakers, in good condition
- if necessary, strongly support your ankles, e.g. use rigid taping
- get medical advice quickly if hurt
- know some first aid
- know your limits—try your hardest, but don't go too far
- be positive in your thinking and behaviour
- avoid dangerous play

- never use alcohol or other drugs before or during physical activity
- cooperate with others in the team
- know and obey the rules
- obey the referee's or umpire's decision, even if you disagree with it
- make sure all fixtures near the playing area are safe, e.g. goal posts are secure and won't fall over
- check that the playing area is level with no holes or dips
- clear away all rubbish, stones, sticks, etc.
- make sure spectators are kept well back from the edge of the playing area, and do not enter the area at any time
- warn spectators and other participants about possible flying implements, e.g. the discus, at a Track and Field Carnival
- keep water, ice, clean cloths, and a first aid kit close to the playing area

Stretching

It is well known that stretching before any physical activity will greatly reduce the risk of body injury. When taking part in an activity, your muscles are about to be put to use. They need to be prepared for the business of contracting (shortening when working) and relaxing (lengthening to normal length). If they contract too quickly, they can easily tear and bleed. This is painful, stops you from doing the activity, and takes days or even months to heal if not treated properly.

A 'cold' muscle needs to be 'warmed-up', even in a hot climate. A quick walk or a slow jog for a few minutes, as well as playing a short minor game without too much twisting or rapid movements, can redirect much of the body's blood to the muscles which need oxygen for movement.

Slow, careful stretches of each set of muscles will help lengthen the muscle and tendon in preparation for your activity. Never bounce or jerk the stretch. Stretching helps relax the muscle, improves blood circulation, and improves performance.

Large muscles (like the thighs) should be stretched and held for up to 30 seconds. Smaller muscles (like the wrist or neck) should be held for up to 10 seconds. Count out loud while you hold the stretch. The muscle should feel uncomfortable but not painful. If it does, ease back on the stretch a little. Most students have already learned to stretch *before* the activity. But some don't realise that it is important to stretch *after* the activity, also. The muscles tend to shorten, or contract because of exercise, and so may be quite sore afterwards. Stretching at the end of the activity helps prevent soreness, promotes (makes better or improves) quick recovery, and helps you to be ready earlier for your next activity.

Reminder:
1. Warm up before stretching
2. Stretch before and after the activity
3. Stretch each set of muscles to be used
4. Stretch gently and slowly
5. Never bounce or stretch rapidly

6. Stretch to the point of tension or discomfort but never pain
7. Breathe slowly and regularly throughout stretching—do not hold your breath.

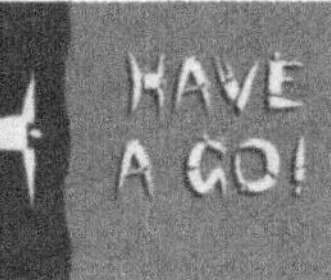

HAVE A GO!

Some stretches are shown in the following photographs. Warm-up first by walking or jogging, and then try some of these stretches. Talk with a partner about which muscles you are stretching.

Figure 5.1 Different stretches for you to try

First aid

The next most important thing you need to know is what to do if someone is injured, especially if the life of the casualty (victim) is at risk. You need to be able to assess (estimate or determine) the level or extent of the injury. You might be the person to have to give help first. This is called first aid. When giving first aid to someone who is hurt and injured (a casualty), you aim to:

- provide a safe environment for the casualty
- preserve life
- prevent the injury or illness from getting worse
- help the casualty to recover
- protect the casualty if unconscious
- help them feel safe and comfortable
- prevent further danger and injury to anyone else, including yourself and the casualty

Medical aid should be given by a doctor or a qualified nurse. The first aider should try to get medical aid to the casualty, if necessary, as soon as possible.

DRABC

The following five steps provide the plan of action for the first aider to follow. The letters **DRABC** stand for Danger, Response, Airway, Breathing, Circulation. The following procedure is explained more fully in first aid books. Here are the main points.

1. D—Danger

When first coming across any person you think is hurt, check for any danger to yourself, the casualty, or any bystanders. Make sure no one else gets hurt. You will not be able to help if you are also a casualty. Continue only if it is safe to do so.

2. R—Response

You must check if the injured person is conscious (able to respond to you and talk with you). Gently shake the casualty's shoulders and ask, 'Can you hear me? What is your name?' If the casualty is conscious, check for and look after any bleeding and other injuries. If unconscious, the casualty will be unable to respond, and may therefore be in a life-threatening condition. Turn him/her on the side. Call for help, but do not leave the casualty.

3. A—Airway

Gently tilt the head backwards and open the mouth. Remove any objects that may be blocking the airway. Lift the jaw forwards with your hand to open the mouth a little.

4. B—Breathing

Look for the chest rising and falling. Listen for the sound of breathing. Feel with your cheek, and with your hand on the chest (diaphragm). If the person is breathing, make sure s/he is comfortable, and in a stable side position. Check for bleeding and other injuries. If not breathing, turn him/her onto the back and begin *Expired Air*

Resuscitation (EAR), giving five quick breaths in ten seconds. To do this, keep the casualty's head tilted back, close the nostrils with your fingers, lift the jaw forward with your other hand. Do not press the neck or throat with your hand.

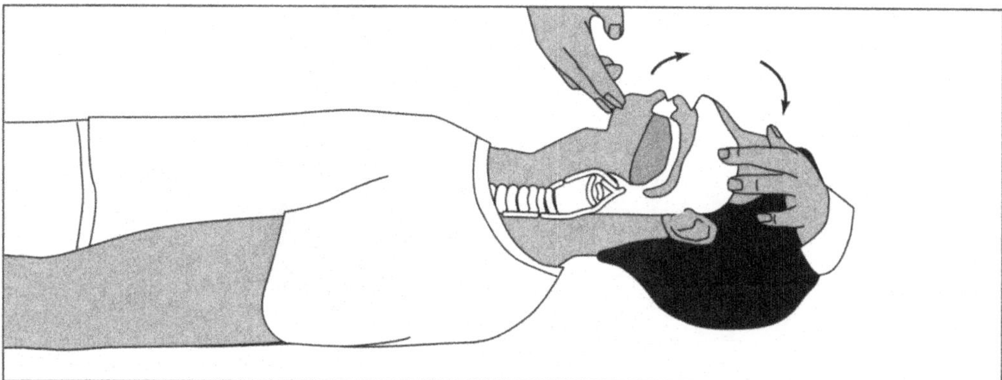

Figure 5.2 Tilt head and open the mouth

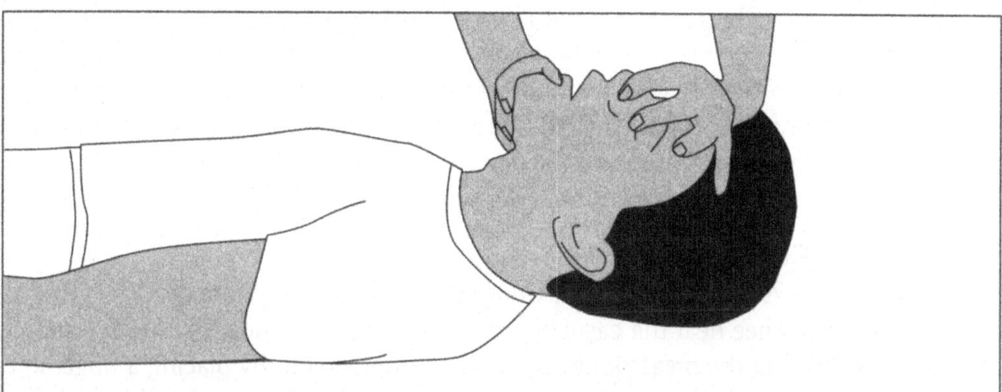

Figure 5.3 EAR

Take a deep breath, place your mouth over the casualty's mouth, and breathe firmly into the casualty's mouth to inflate the lungs. Make sure you have a good seal, and the head is tilted back far enough.

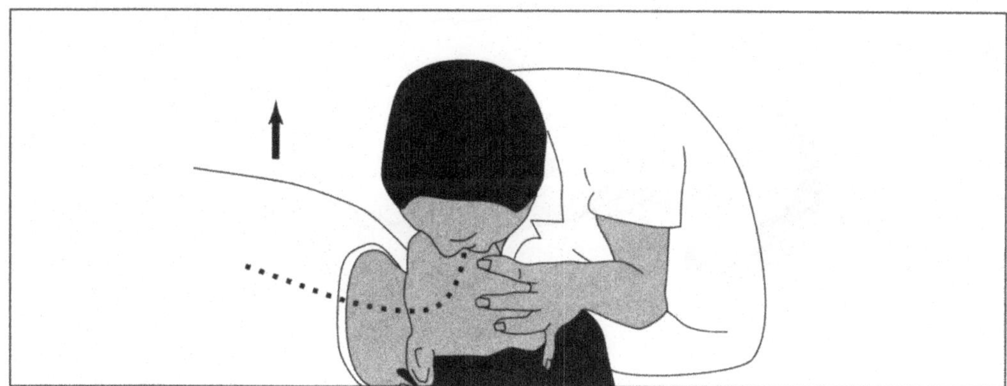

Figure 5.4 EAR

Remove your mouth, turn your head to watch the chest rise and fall. Listen or feel for air being exhaled (breathed out) by the casualty.

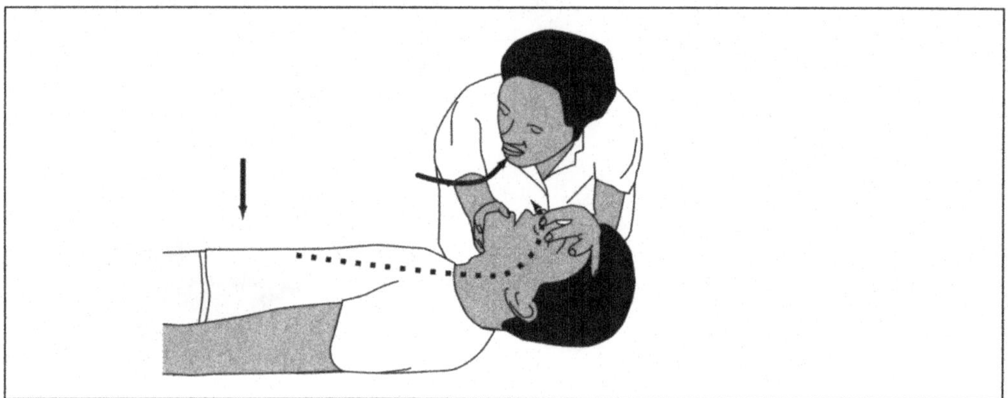

Figure 5.5 EAR

If the chest does not rise and fall, check head tilt position. Then check if something (even the tongue) is blocking the airway. If the airway is blocked, place the casualty on the side to clear it. Give five full breaths in ten seconds, then check the neck pulse. If there is a pulse, continue **EAR** at 15 breaths per minute. If the casualty is a child, the breaths must be gentle, and the rate increased slightly. Breath (count '1, 2, 3, 4') breath (count '1, 2, 3, 4') until about two minutes have passed, then check the pulse again.

5. C—Circulation

If a pulse is not present, start *Cardiopulmonary Resuscitation (CPR)*. To do this kneel with one knee near the casualty's chest and the other near the head. Carefully find the lower end of the breastbone, and then the upper end, by placing a finger in the groove between the collarbones. Spread the thumbs of each hand an equal distance to meet and find the exact middle. Keep the thumb of one hand in that position and place the heel of the other hand below it, on the lower half of the breastbone. Your fingers should be relaxed, pointing across the chest, and slightly raised. Place your other hand securely on top of the first and interlock the fingers.

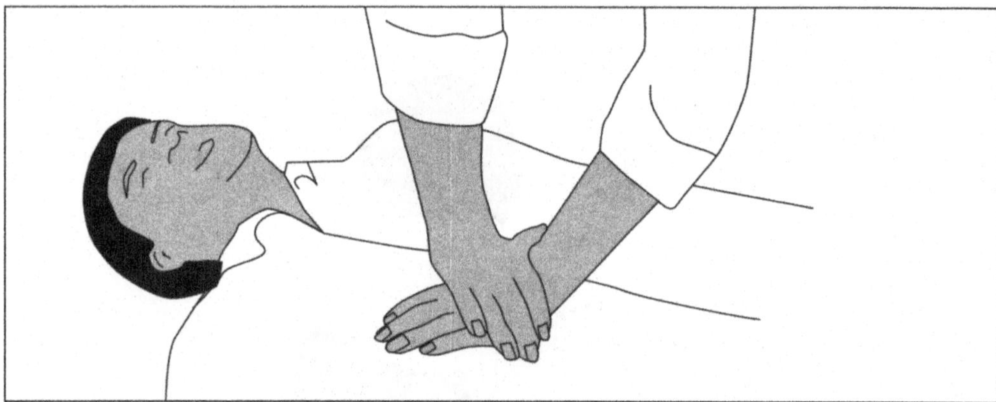

Figure 5.6 CPR

From your upper body, press through the heel of the lower hand. Your shoulders should be above the casualty's breastbone. Keep your arms quite straight. Bend from your hips, and press rhythmically with equal time for pressure and relaxation. Press the breastbone about five centimetres, then relax the pressure. Give 15 presses in 10–12 seconds, then give two breaths in 3–5 seconds. Repeat this pattern four times per minute.

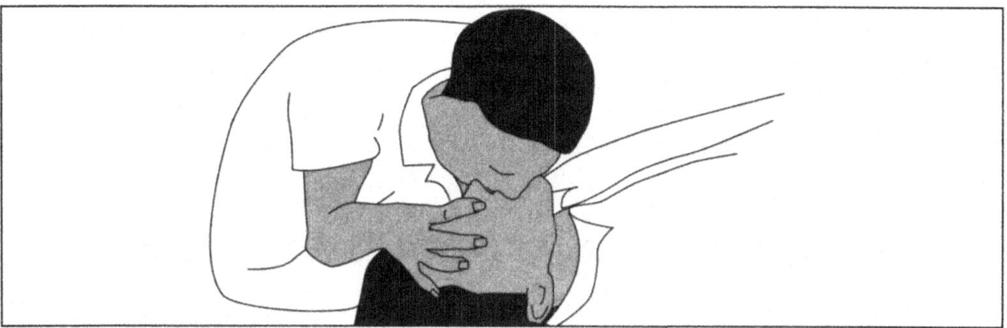

Figure 5.7 CPR

Check every two minutes to see if a pulse has restarted. If carrying out CPR on a child, press much more gently and increase the rate. Keep going for as long as you can, until the casualty recovers, or until medical help arrives. When a casualty regains consciousness, coughing and vomiting may happen, and very quickly. Turn the casualty onto the side so that the airway doesn't become blocked. Leave in a stable side position, lower arm straight out from the body, the upper knee bent at right angles.

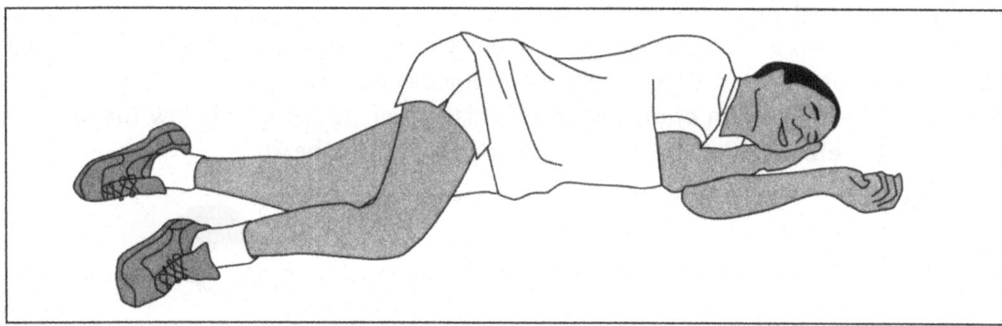

Figure 5.8 Stable body position

Even if done very well, sometimes CPR is unsuccessful because of the cause of the injury or illness, the length of time the casualty has been injured or ill, and the length of time it takes for help to arrive.

Checking the casualty

After looking after life-threatening problems or if such action is unnecessary, what's next?

- Look for any bleeding
- Look for burns or fractures

- Look for soft, sore points, swellings, wounds, or a deformity (loss of proper body shape)

Check the body in this order:

- head and neck
- chest and shoulders
- abdomen and hips
- arms
- legs
- back

Treating common sports injuries

The following are injuries that often happen during physical activity. First aid treatments are listed alongside them.

Soft tissue injuries

Bruises (contusions)

Bruising is probably the most common of all sporting injuries. This is where there is bleeding inside the muscle. It includes a 'corked thigh'. The initials **RICE** are helpful in providing the directions to treating most soft tissue (skin, muscle, and some ligament) injuries where the skin is not broken.

R—**rest** the injured part
I—wrap a little crushed **ice** in a damp cloth, and place it firmly over the injured body part. Very cold water may help if ice is not available.
C—wrap a firm **compression** bandage over, above, and below the injury site
E—**elevate** the site at or above the level of the heart

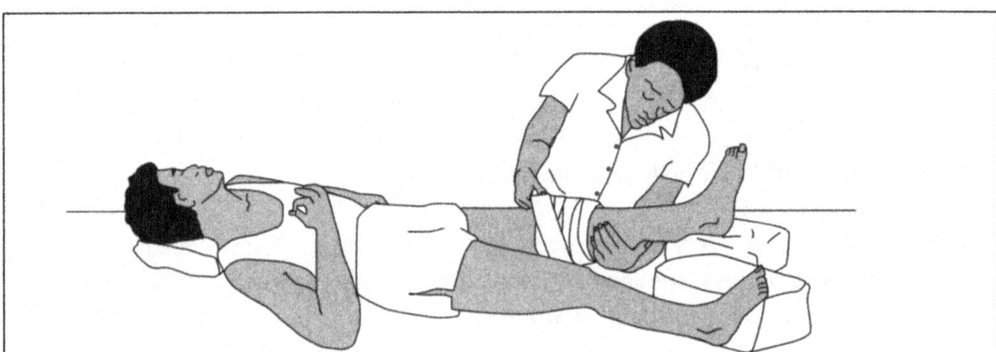

Figure 5.9 Performing **RICE**

Keep the ice on for 20 minutes, then reapply every two hours for the first 24 hours. After a further 24 hours apply ice every four hours. Do *not* rub or massage the injury. Gently, slowly and carefully stretch the muscle along its length, within the limits of pain.

Sprain

This injury happens in many sports such as soccer, rugby, basketball, netball, and softball. The ligaments which hold a joint are torn. It is a painful injury, and movement and function are lost.

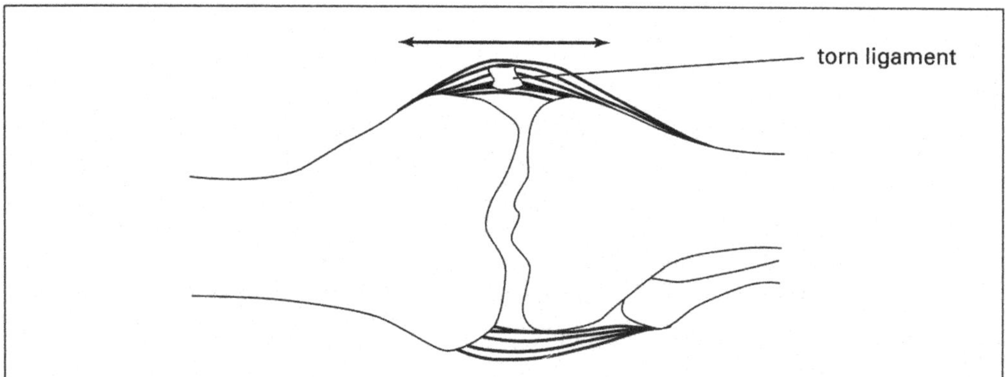

Figure 5.10 Sprain

Use **RICE** and immobilise the joint (make it unable to move) by bandaging and splinting, and get medical help.

Strain

This is an over-stretched muscle or tendon. Use **RICE**.

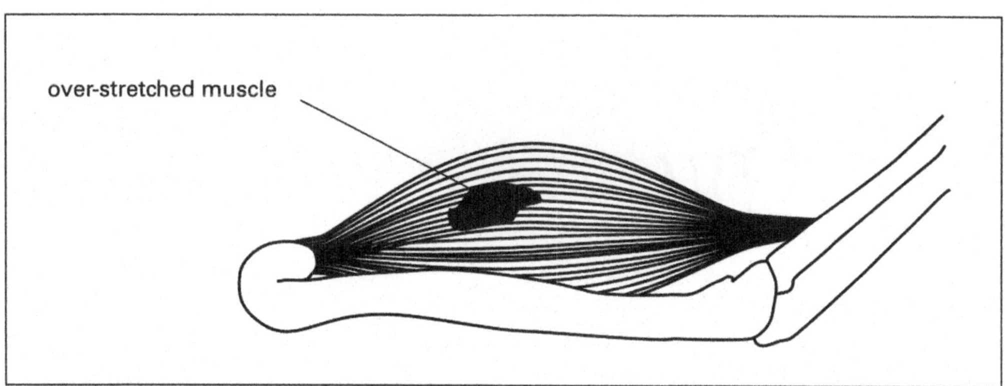

Figure 5.11 Strain

Eye injuries

Avoid rubbing the eye. Don't try to remove anything that may be stuck in the coloured part. Place soft cloth pads over both eyes, lay the casualty on their back with no pressure on the injured eye, advise no eye movement, and get the casualty to medical aid urgently.

If the object is small, loose, and visible:

- it may be washed out with tears
- with the casualty looking up, use the corner of a clean cloth moistened in water
- try washing the eye with a gentle stream of clean water or saline (slightly salty) water

Cramps

Cramps occur when the particular muscle has been overused, jarred, has lost body salt, or has a poor blood supply, e.g. when clothes or boots are too tight. Gently stretch the muscle fully. Apply an ice pack. Do *not* massage the muscle. 'Stitch' is cramping of the muscles of the rib cage or diaphragm, usually when running. The runner should slow down, breathe deeply, and rest.

Winding

This happens a lot in contact sports where the casualty has been hit hard in the upper abdomen. S/he struggles to breathe. Lay the casualty in a comfortable position that assists breathing. Do *not* pump the legs or rub the spot where he was hit.

Groin and testicle injuries

Apply ice packs. Lay the casualty on his back with knees slightly bent, or in a comfortable position. Ask him not to urinate. Get medical help quickly.

External bleeding

Apply direct pressure to the site of bleeding. Place a clean dressing or cloth over the wound. A bigger cloth or pad should be placed over the top of that, and then firmly bandaged. If bleeding continues, change the position of the bigger pad. Place an even bigger cloth pad over the top of that if necessary. Raise and rest the injured part.

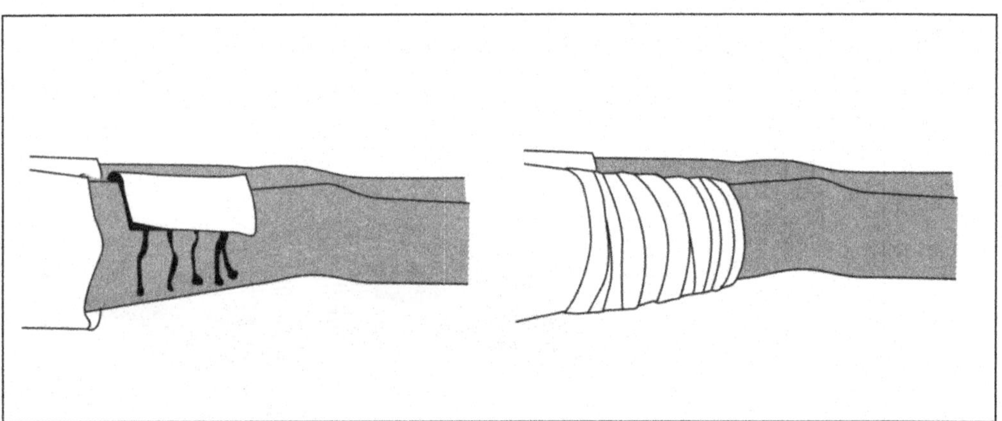

Figure 5.12 Stop the bleeding

Internal bleeding

A casualty may be bleeding from some internal organs. This may be seen by coughing up frothy blood, vomiting with blood in it, or passing urine or faeces which may be streaked with blood. Allow the casualty to rest in a comfortable position. Loosen the clothes, and reassure them. Get medical help urgently. Don't let the casualty eat or drink anything.

Abrasions

The skin is torn as a result of falling on hard or rough ground. The wound may be covered in dirt, and may become infected. Clean the wound thoroughly with a sterile (very clean) cloth soaked in clean or cool boiled water. An antiseptic may be used in the water, or else wash in clean running water. Cover with a dressing or very clean cloth which will not stick to the wound. The first aider's hands should be washed before and after helping the casualty, and s/he should not sneeze, cough or talk while helping the casualty, until the wound is covered. Do not come into contact with the blood or the wound. If something, e.g. a stick is poking from a deep wound, do not try and remove it. Control bleeding by applying pressure to the surrounding areas, but not to the object. Place padding around the object. Get medical help urgently.

Hard tissue injuries

The bones and cartilage of the body can often be hurt in sports, and they take a long time to heal.

Fractures

Fractures of large bones may cause a loss of blood. There is much pain, loss of power and movement at the site, and possible deformity with swelling and bruising. Bandages and/or splints may be used to help support the fractured part.

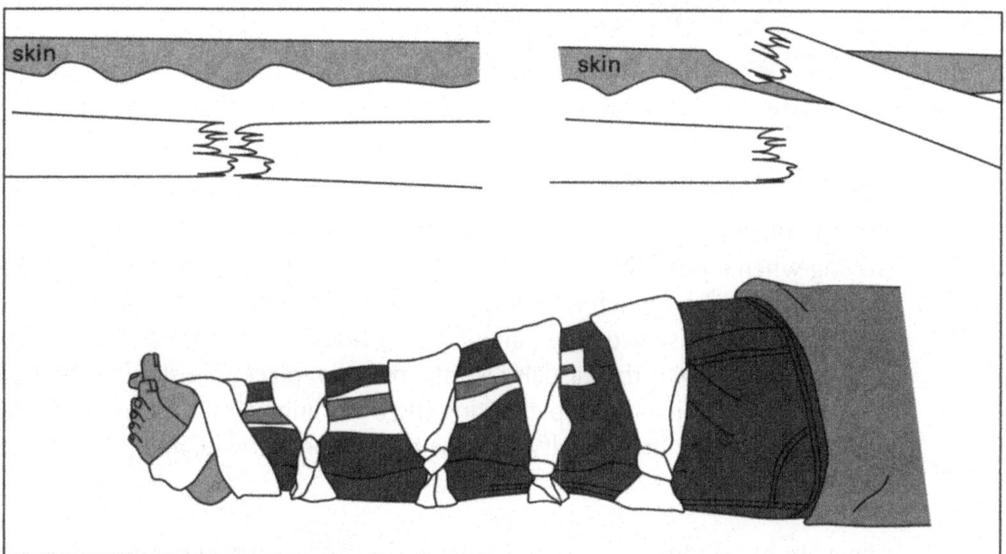

Figure 5.13 Bandages can support the fractured limb

Bandages

Use broad bandages or cloths if possible. Support the limb until the bandages are firmly secured. Regularly check that the bandages are not too tight. They should not be too loose either, so that they support the injured limb.

Splints

Use any firm material that is a little longer than the joints at either end of the broken bone. This could be sticks, thin branches, bamboo, or a school ruler. Provide padding to stop the stick rubbing or cutting into the body. Immobilise (support) the limb by tying broad cloths around the limb and the splint. The limb should not be able to move. Keep knots away from the injury. Get medical help.

Figure 5.14 Using a triangular bandage

Head injuries

Head injuries are very common in sports. Too often a player is allowed to keep on playing when injured, for example, by concussion. Any part of the skull or neck, or the brain, could be hurt when hit heavily. The casualty who has suffered even a mild head injury must be observed very carefully by a doctor or nurse to look for any possible long-lasting injury. If the casualty is unconscious, place in a stable side position with a clear and open airway. Keep checking the breathing and pulse. Support the head and neck while moving the casualty because the neck may be injured. Medical aid must be sought urgently.

There are many more injuries and types of injuries that may happen. The more people who become familiar with first aid procedures, the better.

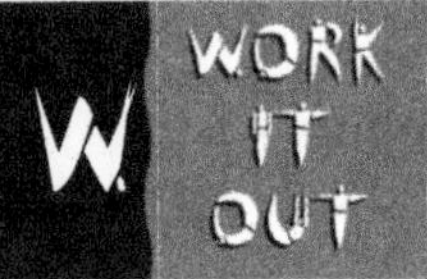

WORK IT OUT!

Answer the following questions and write your answers in your exercise book. Discuss your answers with a friend.

1. What should every person do before and after intense physical activity (such as sport)?
2. List four reasons for providing first aid.
3. Who is qualified to provide medical aid?
4. When providing first aid, what do the initials **DRABC** stand for?
5. When treating soft tissue injuries such as bruises, what do the initials **RICE** stand for?

part two

Taking Part in Physical Activities

- *Traditional Dance and Games*
- *Movement Awareness*
- *Track and Field*
- *Swimming*

6 Traditional Dance and Games

Preview

Traditional dancing helps maintain a good level of fitness, as well as letting people benefit from its social and emotional health components. Throughout Papua New Guinea, there are plenty of opportunities for taking part in traditional dances or singsings. Papua New Guinea is a land of a thousand or more cultures. There isn't enough space to include examples of dances from every region and culture of Papua New Guinea. In this chapter an example of just one people's traditional movement through dance is provided—the Mekeo people of the Central Province.

This chapter also has some traditional games from a number of different provinces. Traditional games in the past have been played mostly in the village but today they also have an important place in Physical Education classes at school. The games can be used as a major part of a lesson or as a warm-up at the start of a lesson.

The history and records of a culture, a community, and its people, is remembered through a range of activities. These include its art, architecture, stories, songs, and poetry. It may also be recorded through movement and physical activity. Nearly all cultures and societies around the world include a variety of movement activities as being an important way of passing on the traditions, and celebrating and remembering that culture. These movement activities may be dances, games, or sports.

Dance

Dances which have been developed within a community are owned by, and are special to that community. They may have a variety of purposes, for example:

- telling traditional stories
- having religious meaning
- having magical meaning
- describing a major event in the history of the community
- celebrating a harvest
- invoking (or requesting) fruitfulness of the harvest or rain, protection, success, and so on.

They may also be purely for pleasure and enjoyment. Because of its importance to society and culture, dance is often taught in schools during Expressive Arts classes. Dance may also be taught as part of Physical Education because it involves many elements of movement activities. As such, it is also considered a healthy movement activity.

If you recall from Chapter Four (Your Fitness), someone who is regularly involved in dance activities, whether traditional or modern, and who wants to dance well, needs to be very fit and healthy.

Dance and appearance

Traditional dance involves a lot more than just the dance. All people enjoy expressing themselves in their personal appearance. The body is like a painter's canvas. Dog's teeth, shell money, shells, facial paint, feathers, tapa cloth, and grass skirts are some of the ornaments. Bright, colourful, joyful body decoration is balanced by careful, controlled body movement. The whole body and its decorations work together in carefully balanced harmony.

Decorated by yellow and red anklets, the feet are grounded, smoothly transferring weight from side to side. Strips of tapa cloth, painted in clan designs, fall from the knees and are seen through the swaying strands of yellow, green, and red grass skirts.

Women interlock their little fingers as they dance, side by side, in a straight line. The goal of the women is to stay in a straight line as they swing their hips in the same direction as the others. If they swing correctly, the grass skirt will stay still in the front, and the back of the skirt will sway to the kundu beats. This is the desired technique of swaying the skirts. Their upper bodies remain still so the designs of the ornaments are displayed. The ornaments tell the story of the dancers' clan and their clan's position in Mekeo society. Who you are, where you come from, and what your clan is known for can all be shown by what you wear.

Mekeo men dress elaborately when taking part in traditional dance. Large head-dresses are worn and the head moves in a nodding motion, rhythmically in time with the beat. As they nod and skip from side to side, the feathers adorning the head-dress wave through the air, fluttering and circling to the rhythm of the kundus. The back of the head is decorated with even more feathers, and strips of coconut leaves hang low to the waist. Strips of yellow patterned tapa hang from the waist emphasising the small graceful steps of the male dancer.

Often men begin a dance by calling out to the others to join them. They circle one another and dance, drum, and sing until enough people arrive to form a large group.

The men organise themselves into long lines facing inwards. The women dance either on the outside of the men in straight lines, or dance within the lines with men to whom they are related. The male dancers move towards each other and meet in the centre before moving back again while drumming and singing. This movement is repeated a number of times.

When they finish dancing they rest, chew betel nut, and talk among themselves. After resting long enough they resume dancing. Mekeo people will dance through the days and into the nights, continuously drumming and singing. The village sleeps with the sound of constant drumming echoing through the sky.

Cultures throughout Melanesia have their own unique style of dance. Young girls and boys join in the dancing with adults. They learn by joining in. Children are encouraged to dance. They are taught songs and dance at their village schools and by their peers. Children enjoy the dances, songs, dress, and decorations of their own people. The dances can be learned, practised, and performed in school at suitable times, so that they may be remembered for always. All of these traditional activities from around the country contribute to the beauty and richness of the nation.

Traditional games

How did you learn to do a task around your house for the first time? Much of our learning takes place by imitation. We learn by watching and copying older people in the village as they go about their day-to-day activities, such as gardening, cooking, and building houses. Just as traditional dances are learnt by imitation, so too are traditional games. They are passed down to each new generation of children. Many different types of games are popular in each province and often reflect the surrounding environment.

Traditional games belong to the community and the people of that community. The games in this chapter were first recorded being taught in schools around 1979 by Oscar Miller, a lecturer at the National Sports Institute. He was visiting schools in different parts of the country, and he understood the importance of traditional games to the community. Have a go at playing these games. Read the instructions carefully first, before you play the game. You may also teach other traditional games from your community to the rest of the class.

'Dibura', or Prisoner (Central Province)

Equipment required: shell
Number of students: any number

How to play

Students sit around in a circle. One student runs around the outside of the circle with a shell in his/her hand. S/he then puts the shell at the back of any of the students sitting around the circle. The student picks up the shell and runs in the opposite direction to the first runner. The two runners run as fast as they can, trying to reach the space left by the second runner.

If the shell is not discovered by the student behind whom it is placed, and the student who left the shell runs around and picks up the shell, then the person behind whom the shell is picked up will have to move into the middle of the circle and s/he becomes a prisoner.

The game continues with changes of students being made by the teacher to provide activity for as many as possible.

'Kaputuu', or Blind Rat and Blind Cat (Bougainville Province)

Equipment required: clean cloth or handkerchief for a blindfold
Number of students: any number

How to play

All students stand in a circle joining hands together. Two are chosen to go into the circle. One is to be the cat and the other to be the rat. They both must be blindfolded with a clean piece of cloth or handkerchief.

The students joining hands should be standing still while the Cat and the Rat are in the circle. While they are in the circle the cat calls out, 'Rat, Rat, where are you?'

The Rat has to clap his/her hands so that the Cat will have to run after it by listening to its clapping sound. The Rat only claps its hands when it hears its name called by the Cat. If the Rat is caught then they change names and the Rat becomes Cat, and the Cat becomes Rat.

'Poki', or Snake (Buin, Bougainville Province)

Equipment required: nil
Number of students: any number

How to play

The students form a single file behind a leader (the 'snake') holding one another with both hands around the waist. Using the snake's movement, students follow the leader wherever s/he goes.

From time to time s/he calls the names of students from the line behind him/her. When a name is called that student must leave the line. When everyone is out of the line, leaving only one at the back of the leader, the leader turns around and makes him/her his/her friend. Both of them chase those who left the line, and try to capture them. The last one to be captured becomes the next leader and the game continues.

Walk, Walk, Walk (East New Britain Province)

Equipment required: nil
Number of students: any number

How to play

The students stand in a circle holding hands. One student is selected to be the first 'walker'. S/he starts trotting around the circle slowly saying, 'Walk, walk, walk'. As soon as s/he touches the back of someone in the circle, s/he stops saying 'walk', and says 'run', and s/he now runs faster. The student touched starts chasing him/her and tries to catch him/her before s/he gets back to the vacant position. If s/he is caught, s/he keeps on running, while the student who has touched goes back to his/her position. S/he continues to run and tries to touch a student and get back to that person's position without being touched. The game continues in the same manner, with the teacher trying to let as many students as possible get a chance to be a 'walker'.

Blind Man (East New Britain Province)

Equipment required: clean cloth or handkerchief
Number of students: any number

How to play

This game can be played during moonlight or during the day. The students form a circle, and one person becomes the 'blind man'. The 'blind man' is in the centre of the circle. S/he first looks carefully around the circle to see and try to remember where each person is standing.

When s/he has done that, the teacher blindfolds the 'blind man'. The teacher gives a signal to the students to move two or three steps either way so that they are no longer in the position they were before.

When asked by the teacher to do so, the 'blind man' moves to find the students. Everyone must be very quiet, because the person who is touched by the 'blind man' will be known if s/he laughs or talks. Other students must not tell the 'blind man' who the person touched is. If the 'blind man' touches a person and says his/her name correctly s/he becomes the blind man. Students change positions each time a new person is picked as the blind man.

'Sae Powate Lumagi Iwiminena' (Western Province)

Equipment required: nil
Number of students: divided into two equal teams

How to play

This game is played by two groups. The students sit in two straight lines about 5 or 6 metres away facing each other. They are given numbers from 1 to as many in the group. The teacher calls a number, for instance, 'Number 6'. The student from each group whose number is 6 gets up and hops on one leg to the centre. When they are both in the centre, still balancing on one leg, they try to bump or knock each other down. They do this using their shoulders. Whoever goes off balance and stands on two legs, or falls down, is out, and the student still balancing on one leg gains a point for his/her team. At the end of the game, whichever team has scored most points is the winner. When calling out numbers of opposing teams, the teacher should:

- consider the size of each student
- consider the sex of each student
- consider the health of each student

'Bolo', or Ball (Central Province)

Equipment required: tennis ball
a wooden bat for each person, about 16 cm wide
cleared area, with a straight line drawn across the centre

Number of students: any number, each with a bat

How to play

This game is played a bit like volleyball, but the ball must be hit over the line drawn in the centre of the cleared area. This line is more or less like a volleyball net. The ball must pass fully over it. A player is allowed to hit the ball only once on his/her side. If the ball is hit back by the opposition, s/he may hit it again. The ball must be hit while it is still moving and before it touches the ground. The side wins a point if the other team is unable to get it back over the line.

7 Movement Awareness

Preview

Movement awareness is a type of gymnastics that concentrates on learning basic movement skills. These skills can be divided into two types:

- locomotor skills, which means the movement takes you somewhere
- stability skills, which help you practise activities such as balancing

Examples of these activities include cartwheels, forward rolls, handstands, somersaults, and handsprings. All you need to perform movement awareness activities is a flat grassy area or, even better, a large foam covered mat. Sometimes proper gymnastics equipment is needed, such as vaults, balance beams, or bars. However if your school doesn't have this equipment there are plenty of activities you can still try.

Movement awareness is important because it helps you develop great sporting skills from a young age, e.g. proper toe-heel landings are practised with the knees bent, and this is how you land after jumping in basketball or after spiking while playing volleyball.

History

Movement awareness has developed from the ancient sport of gymnastics which dates back to ancient civilisations. It was one of the first sports in the Olympic Games and still remains an Olympic event for both men and women. In its beginnings, gymnastics involved a number of acrobatic exercises. These exercises were also used to strengthen soldiers for battles. Later, gymnastics became an important part of the Physical Education programme in schools to help students become strong and healthy. Gymnastics is still part of the school curriculum. Unfortunately, gymnastics is not taught in many schools because there is not enough equipment, and team sports are preferred. It is an exciting part of Physical Education, and, as you will see, can indeed be taught without much equipment.

What is movement awareness?

Gymnastics is sometimes very disciplined, which means everyone must do exactly the same movement at the same time. Movement awareness is more fun and lets everyone work at their own pace, and in their own time. It's a good activity to get into. It helps you learn and develop lots of challenging and exciting activities. These activities include improving your body strength, e.g. standing on your head, improving your flexibility, e.g. doing the splits, and learning new skills, e.g. doing a backwards roll. Sometimes the activities may help you build up courage because they might seem scary the first time you try them, e.g. a handstand forward roll.

Safety rules

All sports need to have safety rules, but the rules are particularly important when practising movement awareness. You need to remember the following:

- concentrate and listen to the teaching points your teacher gives you
- always use a 'spotter': someone who helps you practise the exercise and makes sure you don't fall. Usually they stand at your side.
- work with people your own size
- never stand in the middle of a person's back; stand only on their shoulders
- whenever you are doing rolls, tuck you chin onto your chest so you keep your body (especially your back) rounded
- keep you fingers pointed the way you are travelling

Basic skills

The basic movements can be divided into five different groups as follows:

Travelling

This just means going somewhere and is the first lesson. Skills and movements such as running, jumping, leaping, and skipping are all travelling movements because they take you from one point to another point.

Figure 7.1 Travelling

Balance

Balance is important because it is in every movement you do; even just standing upright requires balance. The best balance position is the 'shoulder width apart' position, e.g. if you are doing a handstand, your hands should be shoulder-width apart on the ground. If you move your hands closer together you'll be unbalanced and fall over.

Figure 7.2 Balancing

Rotation

This means turning and twisting your body into different positions or shapes. A roll is a type of rotation and you can experiment with different types of rolls. Try rolling forwards and backwards in a ball shape, or rolling sideways stretched out in a long position.

Figure 7.3 Forward and backward rolls

Springing and landing

Springing means jumping high into the air and landing is when you come down again. Springing is like letting a curled up spring unwind quickly—it has lots of energy. Landing is also important. Remain balanced, bend the knees, and land lightly on the toes.

Figure 7.4 Bend your knees on landing

Partner work

This means working together to hold a balance activity. Each partner must be strong enough to support someone else's body weight so it's important you choose someone your own size. Partner work can also involve pyramid building and can sometimes require eight or more people in the balance activity.

HAVE A GO!

Try some of the basic skill activities described on the previous pages.
Once you can do them well, you are ready to try the following activities.

Balance

Headstands and handstands are two types of balance activities. To try a handstand follow these teaching points:

Things to remember

- from standing, step forward onto one leg
- put your hands flat on the ground about shoulder-width apart
- at the same time kick your legs up into the air, keeping your arms straight
- balance with your back straight, feet together and toes pointed
- return to the upright position with one foot, then the other.

Handy hints

If you can't maintain your balance, practise against a wall. If that doesn't help, face away from the wall, put your hands on the ground and walk up the wall until you are in a handstand position.

Figure 7.5 Simple handstand

Once you've mastered a simple handstand, get a friend to time you to see how long you can stay up. Then try walking on your hands. You might want to bend your legs for this one. See who can walk the furthest?

Figure 7.6 Can you walk on your hands?

Now try a headstand.

Figure 7.7 Headstand

Rotations

A cartwheel, forward and backward rolls, and swinging around bars, are all types of rotations. Try a cartwheel.

Things to remember

- Use a four placement combination pattern (hand, hand, foot, foot).
- A 'star' style should be kept throughout the movement, finishing with arms extended sideways, facing the other way you started.
- Practise leading with different hands because you'll usually have a preferred side.
- Practise along a line, landing with both hands and feet on the line.

Figure 7.8 Cartwheeling along a line

Advanced cartwheeling skills

- Practise cartwheeling on top of a bench, starting and finishing on top of the bench without falling off (remember to place thick, soft mats on the ground in case you do fall off).
- Practise cartwheeling over a bench by placing one hand on the ground and one on the bench; once over the bench, both feet land on the ground.

Landing

Landing is important in all physical activities because once you go up you must know how to come down. Work with a partner. One person jumps high into the air and uses both feet to land balanced. The second person pushes the shoulder of the jumper when in the air to make sure they are landing in a balanced position. If the jumper wobbles when landing, s/he isn't balanced.

Things to remember

- Land toe first, heel second.
- Land with feet shoulder-width apart.
- Bend the knees to absorb forces.
- Keep your head up.

Figure 7.9 Landing in a balanced position

Springing

Vaulting is jumping quickly and carefully, but with a special method, over a box or hurdle. It is a great way to practise springing. Springing is used to take off at the beginning of a vault.

Things to remember

- Take-off springs are usually double foot springs.
- Hips should be high at take-off.
- Lots of energy is needed.
- Arms should be shoulder-width apart, palms flat with fingers facing forward.

Partner and cooperation work

Partner and cooperative work is really enjoyable. You can try it with even larger numbers of people than are given here. Work with someone your size. Make sure your support base is very stable. Never stand in the middle of a person's back.

Try this

Your partner kneels on hands and knees, pretending their back is a vault. Put one or both hands on the shoulder, and tuck your legs up as you jump across the back. Vault over back. This is a side vault.

Figure 7.10 Side vault with a partner

Try a through vault. Put one hand on your partner's shoulder and one at the base of the spine.

Things to remember

- Never place your hands in the middle of a person's back.
- Work with someone your size.
- Make sure your support base is very stable.
- Keep a reasonable speed through the vault, for good balance.
- Keep your head up, and facing forwards.

8 Track and Field

Preview

Track and field is also known as athletics. Track events include running and they are held on the track. Field events include jumping and throwing, and they are held on the field. Some events require special equipment and are therefore not taught in some schools in Melanesia. Safety rules must be followed when taking part in track and field events.

The *Track* events include all the running events. The main ones are:

sprints	100 metres
	200 metres
	400 metres
middle distance	800 metres
	1500 metres
	3000 metres
long distance	10 000 metres
	marathon, and half marathon
hurdles	110 metres
	400 metres
steeplechase	3000 metres
walking	20 kilometres
relays	4 x 100 metres
	4 x 400 metres

The *Field* events include all the jumping and throwing events. These include:

jumping	high jump
	long jump
	triple jump
	pole vault
throwing	shot put
	discus
	javelin
	hammer

There are also some combined events. In the *men's decathlon* the competitors attempt ten running, jumping, and throwing events (from the previous list) over two consecutive days. They are awarded points according to their placings, times, and distances. The decathlon winner is the individual who has gained the most points by the completion of the tenth event. The women compete in a *heptathlon* taking part in seven track and field events, also over two consecutive days. Women compete in nearly all the same events as men, but may use lighter equipment, the walks are shorter, and the hurdles are lower.

Figure 8.1 Can you name these track and field events?

Track and field in school

You may take part in some track and field events while at school. However, some events are not taught in school because they are considered suitable only for people who are physically mature. Most events can be tried if there is an open, level, safe space for students to run, throw the javelin or discus, or jump for distance or height.

Every student in secondary school should have the chance to learn to perform every possible event. Remember, though, that the school may be unable to teach every event. As you get older, interests and strengths will be different. Some students will run quicker than others. Some will be able to last longer in endurance races. Other participants may not be very fast in sprints or last in long races, but may be able to jump high or over a long distance. Others excel in the throwing events. Track and field is therefore an excellent area of physical learning because there is something for everyone.

It is also important to remember that teachers must teach you well and carefully, especially for your own safety. Fortunately for students in most schools in Papua New Guinea, every qualified Physical Education teacher from the National Sports Institute in Goroka will have had good training to be able to teach you properly and safely. They will also know how to mark out a track and field for the school's use, and how to run a carnival.

Track and field events are best conducted at a carnival. This can be held between classes (groups of students about the same age), between schools in your area, and even against students from other areas, and other countries. Junior or under-age athletics events can be fun and very enjoyable. Every person should be encouraged to take part. Carnivals at the school level should be designed not to have one person first, one person second, etc, but organised so that every participant can show that he or she ran this race faster than the last time s/he ran it; or s/he threw the javelin or discus further than the last time s/he threw it. This approach gives more people more opportunities and greater interest in trying to improve on their own 'personal best'.

When a student reaches the age of 16 or 17, s/he can then choose if s/he wishes to be involved in competitive track and field events. This may first take place in the school carnival, in school houses. A suitable team may then be selected to represent the school against other schools. School sportsteachers and Provincial Recreation Officers may work with the Papua New Guinea Athletics Union to run regional carnivals. Finally a Papua New Guinea National team may be chosen to compete against students of the same age from other countries.

One such carnival for school students is the Pacific School Games. These were first held in Brisbane in 1986, then in Sydney in 1989, and Darwin in 1992. Students from Papua New Guinea have competed well against representatives from many other nations, including New Zealand, Japan, China, Canada, Fiji, and even Europe. It is a very exciting time for them!

Figure 8.2 Elanga Buala performing the Fosbury Flop at the Pacific School Games in Brisbane

Major international events

Every two years the World Athletics Championships are held at a major international stadium. The fifth world championships were held in Gothenburg, Sweden, in 1995, and in 1997 in Athens, Greece.

Perhaps the highest point of achievement in track and field, however, is to take part in the biggest regular sporting event in the world's history. This is the Olympic Games. The Olympic Games began on a running track and throwing field, over 2000 years ago in Greece. It was a celebration of the people's skills, to the Greek gods on the sacred Mount Olympus.

Today, these games are held in a selected city somewhere around the world, every four years. In 1988 they were held in Seoul, South Korea; in 1992, Barcelona, in Spain; in 1996, Atlanta, U.S.A. In the year 2000, they are being held in Sydney, Australia, and in 2004 they will be held in the original city of the ancient Olympics, Athens, in Greece.

Track and field

Let's now look at some of the different track and field events. Some suggestions to help you in each event are provided in this book. Your library may also have more detailed books with diagrams to help you learn more about each event you do in your PE class, or in preparation for your school carnival.

It is important to remember information you have read in earlier chapters, such as Your Fitness and Sports Injuries, in preparing you for track and field events. Before doing any event such as sprinting or high jumping, it is necessary that your body, especially the muscles, are ready to take part in these events. You must carefully warm up, and stretch your muscles to prepare for the hard work that they are about to do. Otherwise your muscles may stretch too fast and tear. Then, you can't do anything until you are completely healed. Plus, it's painful!

Some events such as pole vault, hammer throw, the steeplechase, and the decathlon, are not detailed here because they are not often included in school carnivals.

Running events

100 metres

The track is straight, with narrow painted lanes of 33 cm width. It is important to get a good start, especially if you are running in bare feet on a surface which is smooth or slippery, like grass. The difference between winning and losing is often being able to maintain high speed until past the finishing line, and not slowing towards the end. Lean your chest towards the finishing tape.

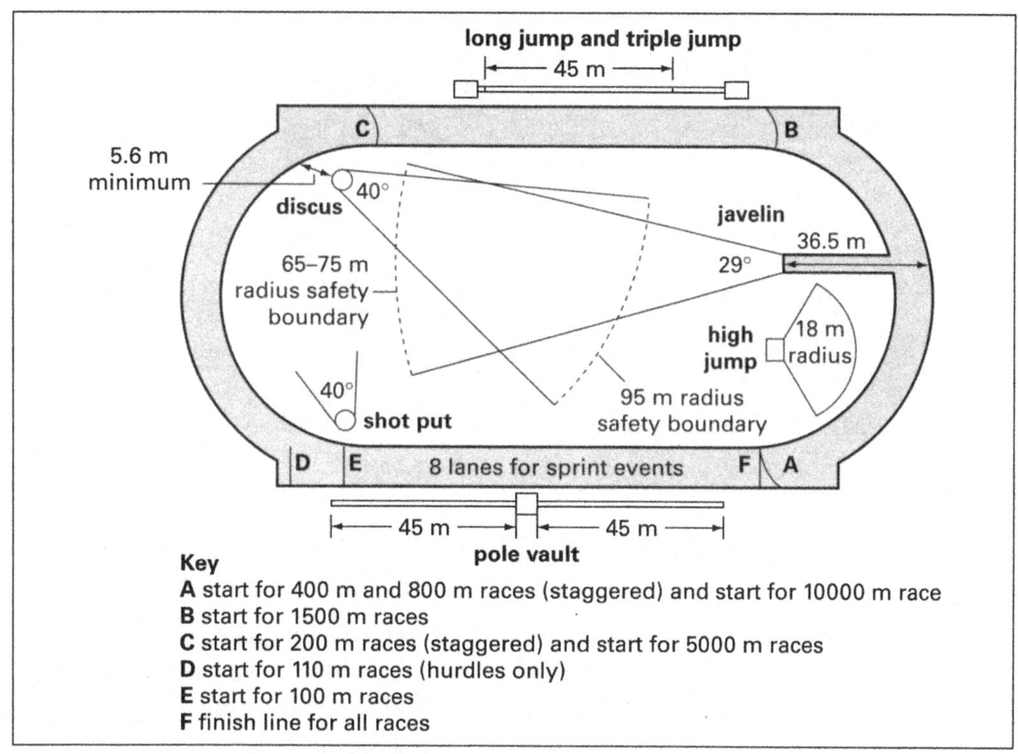

Figure 8.3 Layout of an athletics track

Figure 8.4 Running

The world record (**WR**) is:
Men 9.85 secs (1994); Women 10.49 secs (1988)
(The world records which are noted for each event were current in 1995.)

200 metres

The start is on a curve, and everyone has a staggered starting point (different position) because of the curve. You finish on the straight. You must stay in your lane and not cross the line.

Figure 8.5 You must stay in lane until the race is finished

WR: Men 19.72 secs (1979); Women 21.34 secs (1988)

400 metres

Most running tracks are 400 metres long, with two straights of equal length and two equal curved ends. This event goes around the track once. It has a staggered start so that everyone runs the same distance, to finish at the end of the straight. Again all competitors must stay in their own lanes for the whole distance.

Figure 8.6 400 metres race

WR: Men 43.29 secs (1988); Women 47.60 secs (1985)

800 metres

This event is a middle distance event which requires two circuits of the 400 m track. Runners are spread across the track behind a slightly curved line to start, and must stay in lanes until they reach the end of the opening curve (for about 40 m) before they are permitted to cross into the inside lane. The inside lane is the shortest distance and therefore the quickest track to take.

WR: Men 1:41.73 mins (1981); Women 1:53.28 mins (1983)

1500 metres

Just under four laps of the 400 m track make up the 1500 m race. It starts in the same way as the 800 m race. The race must be carefully planned so that the runner has enough energy and strength left for a final quick burst to the finish.

WR: Men 3:27.37 mins (1995); Women 3:50.46 mins (1993)

3000 metres

This is usually the longest race conducted in high schools. It takes just under eight laps of the running track and requires runners to keep a steady speed over the whole distance. Again, it is important to keep an energy reserve for the conclusion of the race. Sometimes, runners who have led most of the race finish well back in the field, overtaken by those who have used the leader's pace as a guide, then simply overtaken the leader in the final 200 m. These long distance events need great mental courage and strategy, physical endurance and fitness.

WR: Men 7:25.11 mins (1994); Women 8:06.11 mins (1993)

Relays

Relays comprise teams of four runners, and the most common distances run are 100 m or 400 m for each person. The first runner carries a baton to the next person in the team waiting in position, passing it within a short marked space within the lane. The baton is an aluminium tube which is passed by hand to the hand of the next runner. The speed, accuracy, and timing of the pass are essential for success, combined with commencing the run.

For the **4x400 m relay**, the first runner of each team must stay in lane for the first lap. When the baton is passed to the 2nd, then the 3rd and the 4th runner, these runners are not required to stay in that lane; they move into the shortest path, which is on the inside lane. However they must be very careful to avoid all interference with other runners at the changeover.

The **4x100 m relay** is possibly the most exciting race of all to watch. The runners must stay in their lanes and not cross outside the line because they might interfere with another runner. The baton has to be passed within a marked area of 20 m. If dropped, it has to be picked up again; dropping the baton usually means too much loss of time and place. Several judges are required at each change to watch the changeover.

Walking

This event has very few participants in Melanesia. This is unusual because it is an event where competitors could do very well, including in schools. There are two particular rules in the walking technique which are very closely watched:

- The back leg must be fully straightened in its upright phase
- The heel of the front foot must contact the ground before the back foot leaves the ground

Unlike running there is no fully airborne phase where the athlete is in the air, and there is no ground contact. There must always be some ground contact. To get the best possible drive for power (and maintain balance), walkers pump their arms hard across their bodies, driving energy through their hips. This gives walking an unusual swinging hips kind of walk, but is very quick over long distances.

Marathon

This is one of the most famous races of all. Its distance is just over 42 kilometres. This represents the distance a Greek messenger ran from the town of Marathon to the city of Athens, to tell of the defeat of the Persian armies at the Plain of Marathon.

The athletes who enter this event have trained for several years by running many kilometres, often over 100 kilometres per week. Therefore it is unsuitable for school students. Only a few well-trained and coached runners should try it.

The best winning times from around the world are about 2 hours 07 minutes for men (1988), and 2 hours 21 minutes for women (1985).

Jumping events

High jump

Jumpers are required to jump as high as possible over a horizontal bar supported by two vertical poles. The two vertical poles have small movable platforms, on which the long horizontal bar is placed. Jumpers approach the bar from any position, jump off one foot only (or else it is a foul), and must clear the bar without knocking it off (even though it may be touched during the jump). A soft, thick (about 80 cm or more) mat is placed behind the bar for the jumper to land on. The height of the bar is measured at the centre, where it dips a little. To jump over the bar, three types of jumps may be used.

1. Scissors kick—a straight approach is needed, with a high kick of the leading leg, followed with a high kick of the other leg.

Figure 8.7 Scissors kick

2. Western roll—a slightly curving approach is needed, with the leading leg kicked high as the jumper rolls over the top. As the jumper lays out flat along the bar s/he rolls over the bar with arms above the head, and then drops down onto the mat.
3. Fosbury flop—named after the first jumper to develop this style, it is the most successful technique for those jumpers reaching the highest heights. It has a 'J' shaped approach, and as the jumper nears the closest upright, the nearest knee is driven up and across the body to the opposite shoulder, at the same time driving the arms upwards for lift. The trailing foot pivots on the ground, causing the body to rotate on the way up and to cross the bar, shoulder first. The heels are kicked up as they cross the bar, and the jumper relaxes to land on the mat, on the shoulders and upper back. Heights of over two metres have been cleared using the Fosbury flop method, even by high school students. Students doing scissors can clear about 1.4 m, but it is very difficult to get any higher, even for the best athlete.

Figure 8.8 The Fosbury flop

The best high jumpers are people who have a tall, slim build. Timing and confidence are all very important in this event. However there is a risk of serious back and neck injuries upon landing. Only attempt high jumps when a good landing mat is in place, and in the correct position.

Three attempts are permitted, but a jumper is out when three 'fails' are eventually recorded on one height.

WR: Men 2.45 m (1993); Women 2.09 m (1987)

Long jump

Success in this event combines running speed on the approach track with an explosive jump for height, as well as distance. The run-up must be very carefully marked out, to take off on the take-off board without fouling by stepping over. The board may have a little sand scattered on it to see if a toe has crossed it. Sometimes plasticine may also be used.

The whole body must be used to leap powerfully for height in the actual jump. While in the air, prepare for landing by reaching both legs as far forwards as possible. The distance is measured from the mark left by your body in the sand nearest the take-off board, so don't put your hand back behind you as you get up!

The landing pit should be filled with soft, clean, freshly raked and loose sand. The surface should be very smooth and level, smoothed after each jump. The take-off board is set level in the ground, a little (about one metre) back from the front edge of the pit. The runway is smooth and is clear, like the running track, and is free from any obstacles.
WR: Men 8.96 m (1995); Women 7.52 m (1988)

Triple jump

The take-off board for the triple jump (also known as the 'hop, step, and jump') is set much further away from the landing pit; it can be six, eight, or ten metres from the edge. This is to allow jumpers to do the first two parts of the event on firm ground before the third part (the jump) allows them to land in the sand. Like the long jump, the run-up must be very carefully measured out by each competitor. This will allow them to commence the first part of the event as close to the take-off board as possible. The event has three consecutive parts: the hop, the step, the jump.

- the hop—take off from the board from one leg and land on the *same* leg
- the step—continue into the air to land on the *other* leg
- the jump—now take off as high as possible into the air like the long jump and land on both legs in the pit.

It is sometimes helpful to say the movements to yourself to help the initial confusion, e.g. 'same, same, other, together' with each movement. Or you could call the side used as you do them. Three attempts are recorded in this event, and the best distance wins.
WR: Men 18.29 m (1995); Women 15.50 m (1995)

Throwing events

These events were based upon the use of various weapons during war time. Because of this, these events can be dangerous if safety rules are not followed. Always listen to the teacher's instructions and never point or throw the implements (equipment) at or towards anyone.

Shot put

The 'shot' in the shot put is based upon a cannon ball, fired from large guns in old European armies and on old sailing ships. The shot used in secondary schools weighs 3 kilograms for boys and 2.5 kilograms for girls. To *put* the shot is definitely not throwing it; the shot is purposefully too heavy to throw. To try to throw it would damage ligaments and tendons in your elbow and shoulder joints.

Stand at the back of the 2.135 metre diameter circle. Don't step out of the circle until your attempt is completed, then leave from the back. Stand sideways, with your putting shoulder away from the direction the shot will travel. Place the shot in your fingers (not your palm). To start, rest the shot against your cheek. Your body is coiled, like a spring. Your feet step, slide together, and step towards the front edge of the circle. To propel (push) the shot, you must quickly uncoil, or use your whole body like a snake striking. Your legs, back, shoulders, arms and fingers must push and release the shot extremely powerfully (using speed and strength). Watch the trajectory (path, flight, or direction) of the shot. If it's too high it won't carry through the air and if it's too flat, it will fall to the ground quickly because of its weight.

WR: Men 23.12 m (1990); Women 22.63 m (1987)

Figure 8.9 Putting the shot

Discus

The discus is a 1 to 1.5 kg weapon designed in the days of the ancient Greeks. Shaped like two plates on top of each other, it spins out of the front of the hand and can travel great distances, if it doesn't wobble.

The thrower enters the 2.50 m diameter circle and stands, holding the discus away from the direction of the throw. It rests on the tips of the fingers, which are slightly bent. It is not gripped in the fingers, nor by the thumb. The thrower begins a balanced wind-up, the hand holding the discus balanced by the opposite arm held out and up.

Figure 8.10 Aliti O'Keeffe preparing to throw the discus

Starting low and slightly crouched, the release is as high as possible in the direction of the throw, allowing the discus to carry as far as possible. The carrying arm is kept very slightly bent during preparation, and is straightened at release. The thumb leads the way. At the point of release, the discus spins out past the first finger. A skilful thrower can spin once or twice in the circle to have greater speed to deliver the discus.

Note that this event can be very dangerous because the discus can easily slip out of the hand, especially if the thrower uses the spin. A safety net like a cage or high fence is used in major competitions to protect officials or others nearby. If this can't be provided, then everyone must be clearly warned to stand well back from the thrower, and watch where the discus travels.

WR: Men 74.08 m (1986); Women 68.72 m (1994).

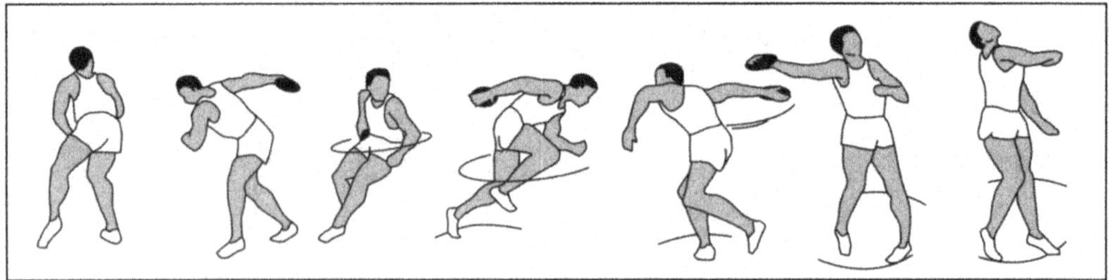

Figure 8.11 Throwing the discus

Javelin

The javelin is a specially weighted spear, designed to be thrown over long distances. Secondary students use a javelin weighing about 800 g.

When preparing to throw the javelin, it is important to place your fingers correctly on or against the rope grip. Run quickly to the throw line, but do not cross it! During the last few steps your upper body rotates in order to be side-on to the line for the throw. The javelin is held lightly in your throwing fingers; it must not be held so tightly that it swings about. The point is held up at the angle that the javelin will be thrown. The throwing action uses the whole body, placed sideways, with the throwing arm at the back. The front arm starts high to balance the whole body. This action requires speed and power.

WR: Men 95.66 m (1993); Women 80.00 m (1988)

Figure 8.12 Throwing the javelin

9 Swimming

Preview

Swimming has played an important role in all societies and on all continents, not just as a sport, but as a useful practice and leisure activity, especially where people live near lakes, rivers, or oceans.

In western society, illustrations from ancient Egyptian times show how widespread swimming was. For the Greeks the swimming 'pond' was the most important part of the gymnasium. Swimming also played a vital role in the military training of young men. Swimming has became an important component of physical training for children all over the world. The main swimming strokes learnt include the front-crawl, the back-crawl, the breast-stroke, and the butterfly stroke. Safety in the water needs to be fully understood and practised by everyone.

History

Swimming became an Olympic event in 1896. The side-stroke and breast-stroke were the first techniques developed. In 1906 an Australian named Healy showed a new crawl technique during a swimming festival in Germany. This became the crawl-stroke and has survived, basically unchanged, to this day. The early back-stroke incorporated a breast-stroke kick with arms being brought out sideways and outward. This slowly changed to the back-crawl we know today. The development of the butterfly stroke started in 1930, but the dolphin kick was only approved in competitions in 1953. Swimmers used a racing dive to start for the first time in 1912. Before this time, all races started in the water and this continued until 1920. The start from the blocks was first used in the 1936 Olympic Games.

Figure 9.1 Take your marks, go!

The aquatic environment and safety

Swimming can take place in many different environments. In Melanesia the following settings are most evident.

Streams and rivers

In these aquatic environments it is important for the swimmer to:

- check the water depth
- check for underwater dangers
- explore by wading before swimming
- keep away from strong currents
- swim diagonally downstream if caught in a current
- assist others where possible

Figure 9.2 Children playing in the river

Sea

In this situation it is important for the swimmer to:

- never swim alone
- study how the waves are breaking before you enter the water
- ask local people about the beach conditions
- constantly check your position when in the water so as not to drift too far
- float or swim diagonally out if caught in a current
- try to signal somebody by raising one arm if being carried out to sea
- keep away from rocks
- dive under large waves
- not interfere with unknown sea life

Figure 9.3 Playing on the beach

Dams, reservoirs, lagoons

In these situations it is important to:

- keep away from the edge
- remain calm, try to float and, if tangled in weed, gently pull it away
- if you see someone in difficulty, try and assist by reaching out with a stick or branch, your arm, or clothing or towels tied together.

Boats

Boat travel is responsible for many tragedies because of overloading, unsteadiness leaks, the boat being too small for the intended use, or alcohol-use by the occupants It is important to:

- check the boat for leaks
- check the boat for necessary safety equipment
- test for stability
- keep your weight as low as possible and do not stand up
- stay near the boat if it capsizes
- do not drink alcohol while in the boat

Swimming pools

In this situation it is important for the swimmer to:

- not dive into shallow water
- not jump on other swimmers
- keep out of the deep water if not confident

Figure 9.4 Taking care on the boat

- keep close to the edge until confident
- walk around the pool edge and never run
- learn to swim well
- leave the water when feeling cold or tired
- not push others in

The swimming strokes

Swimming offers a variety of opportunities for all people to take part in physical activity, regardless of age, sex, or performance standards. The formal swimming strokes include the following.

Freestyle, or front-crawl

In this stroke the swimmer lies on top of the water on the stomach. The arms move around in a circular motion while the legs kick up and down in a flutter kick. As one arm pull nears completion, the head is rotated to the side for breathing. The breath is taken as the arm leaves the water and inhalation or air is taken in through the mouth.

1. As one arm begins the pull with the elbow straight, the other arm begins its recovery by bending and lifting the elbow upward. The legs kick up and down in a flutter kick.
2. The pulling arm bends at the elbow. As it is pulled under the body the elbow is held high.

Figure 9.5 Sir Donald Cleland swimming pool, Port Moresby

3. The pulling arm reaches maximum elbow bend as it passes under the shoulder and chest. The recovering arm enters the water directly in front of the shoulder.
4. As the arm pull nears completion, the head is rotated to the side for breathing.
5. A breath is taken in through the mouth as the arm leaves the water.

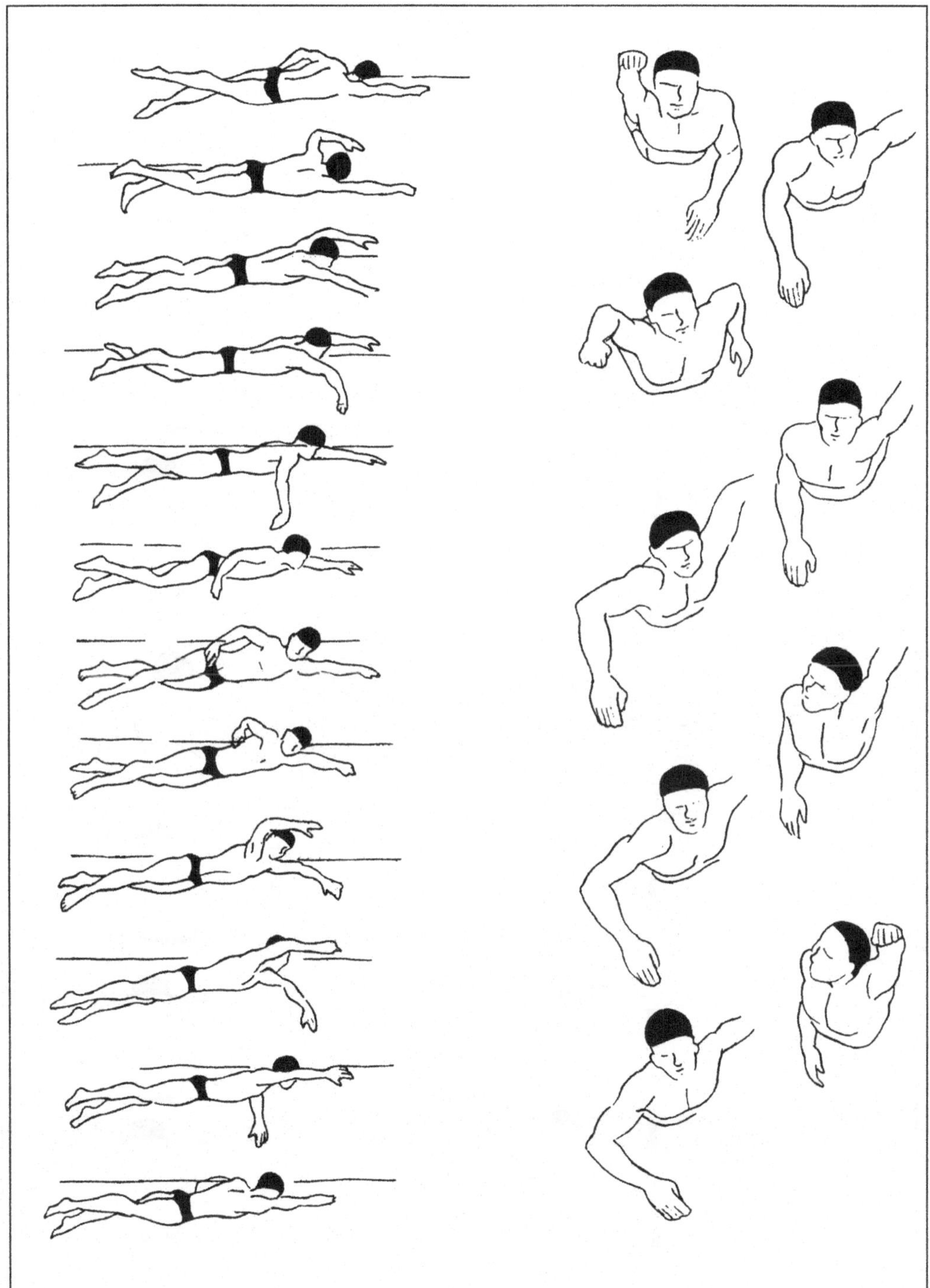

Figure 9.6 Front-crawl

Back-stroke or back-crawl

In this stroke the swimmer lies on the back in the water. It is important to keep the chest up. The arm enters the water at a point directly over the shoulder. The legs are kicked up and down in a flutter kick. As one arm sinks downward as the pull begins, the other arm starts its recovery directly upwards.

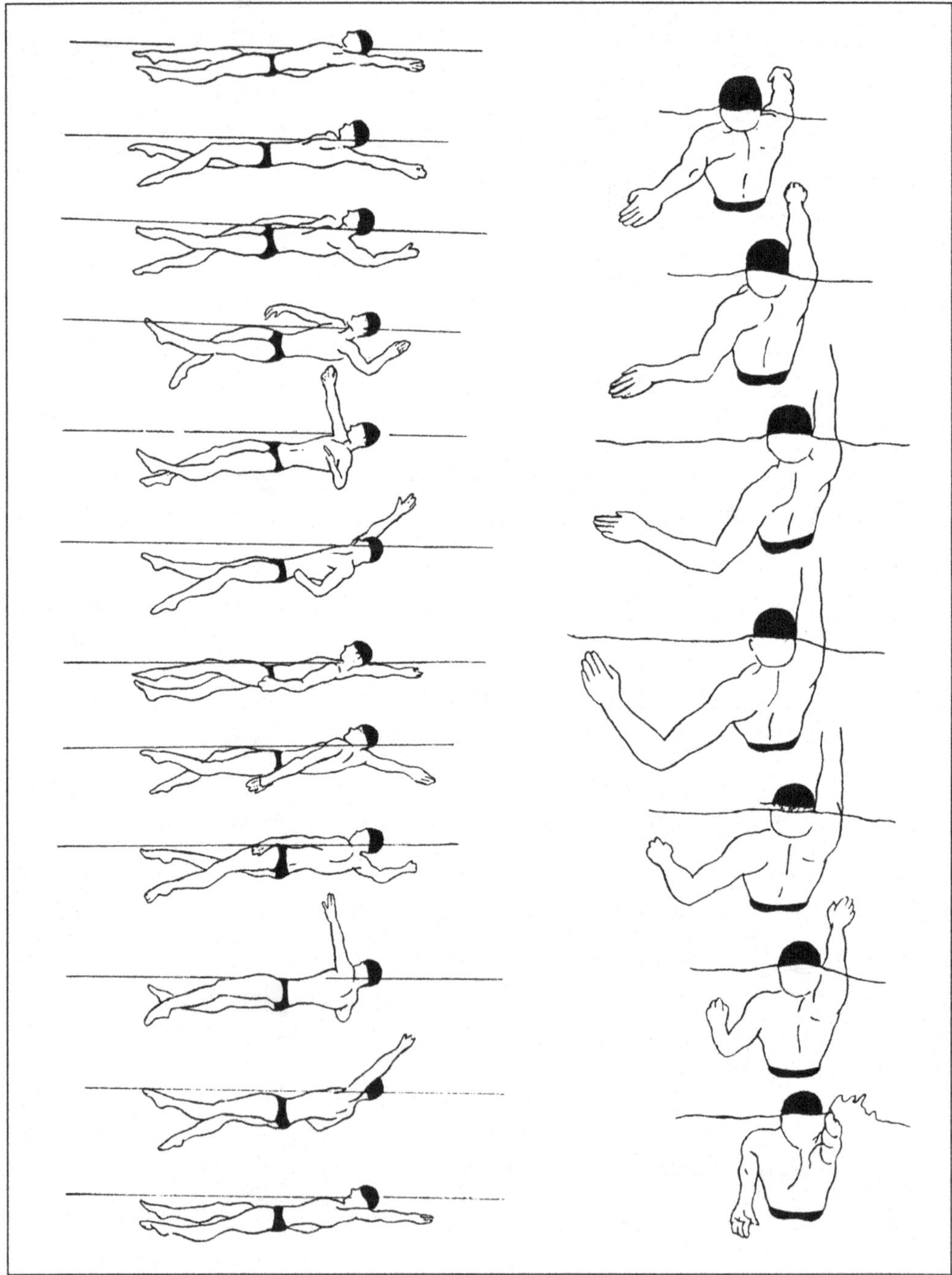

Figure 9.7 Back-crawl

Breast-stroke

In this stroke the swimmer begins on the stomach in a stretched-out, horizontal position. The arms are pulled outwards, downwards and back. The head is lifted up as the arms are pulled in towards the chest. A breath is taken and at this time the legs are bending up. After the breath is taken, the face is placed back into the water and the arms are pressed forward.

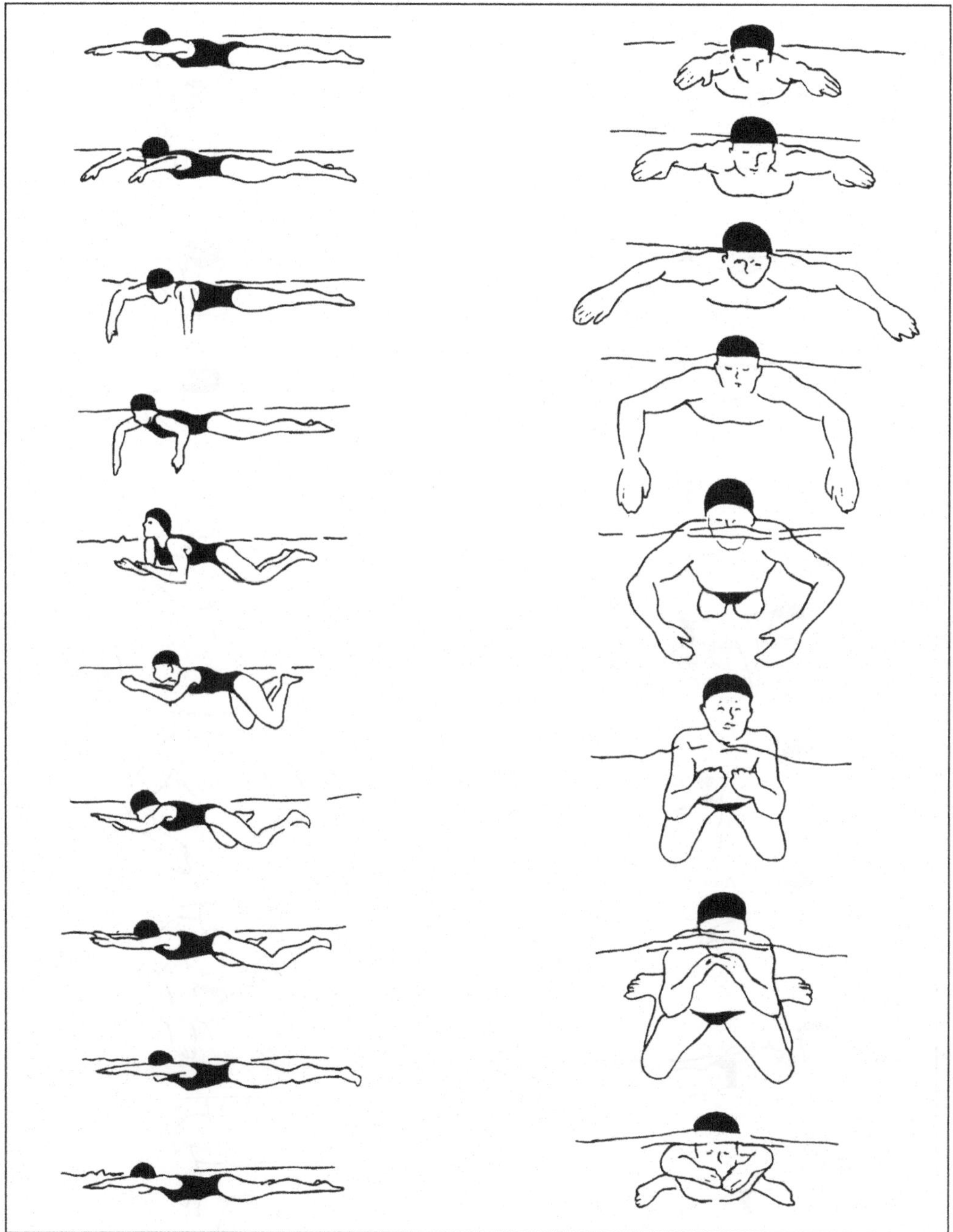

Figure 9.8 Breast-stroke

Butterfly

In this stroke the swimmer begins on the stomach. Both hands enter the water at the same time, shoulder-width, with the elbows straight. The feet kick downwards, working together. The hands press in, outward, and downwards, with the elbows held high and bent. Hands come close together under the chest and are bent at right angles. Arms finish the pull, a second kick is made, and the breath is taken. Arms are recovered over the water and the head is lowered so the face is down.

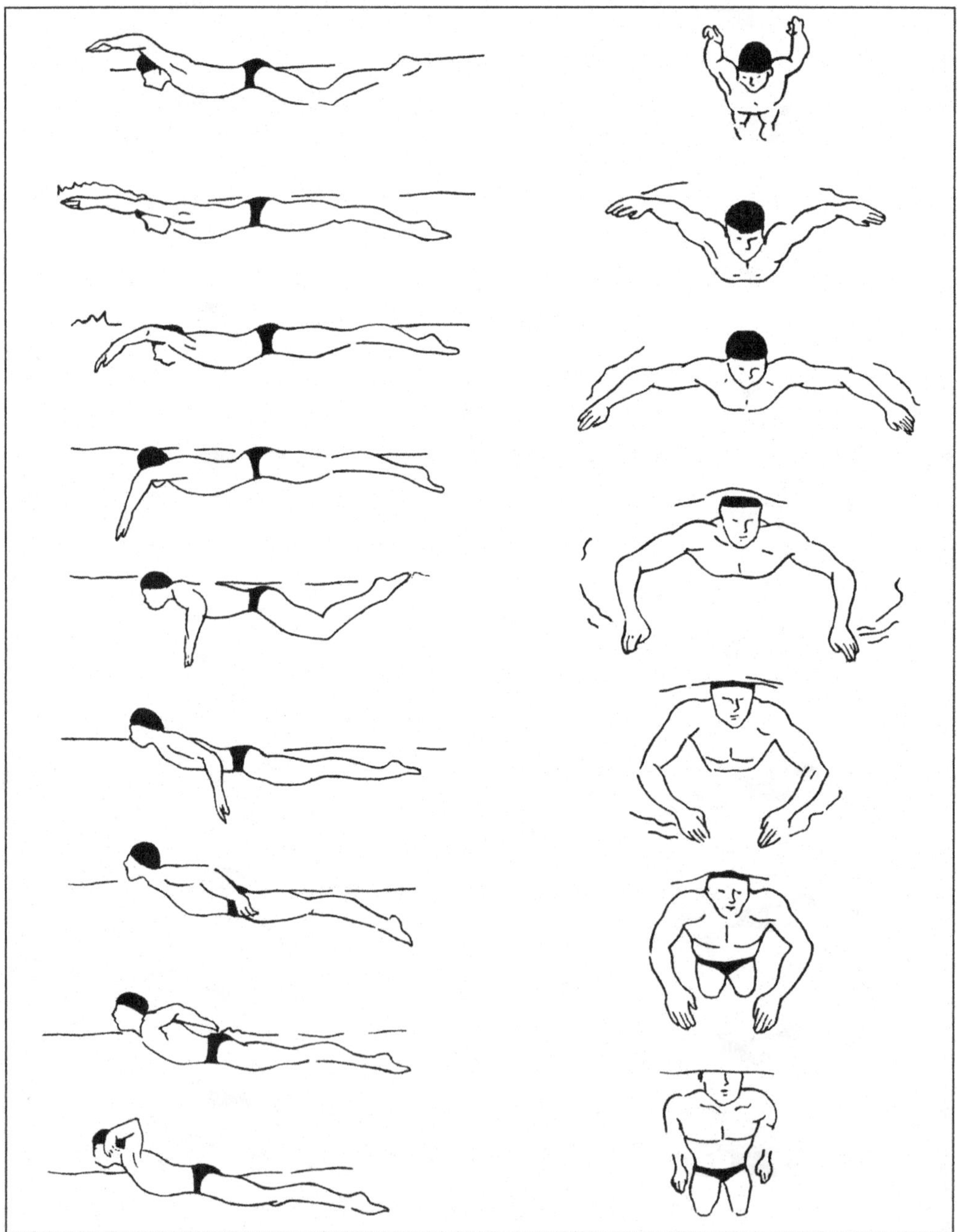

Figure 9.9 Butterfly

Other strokes

The informal swimming strokes include the following.

Survival back-stroke

A breast-stroke kick is performed with the swimmer on the back. The forearms are bent and move from the shoulders down to the hips. The stroke finishes with a short glide with the legs together and the arms beside the body.

Side-stroke

This may be performed on either side of the body. The body is stretched out on its side in a streamlined position. There is a bend at the hips and knees with legs and feet together. The top arm begins to pull down and the bottom arm recovers upwards. Open the legs by moving the top leg forwards and the bottom leg backwards. The bottom arm starts to pull downwards, while the top arm starts its recovery. Then the legs are brought forcefully together and a glide occurs.

Survival

It is essential, particularly in a country where few schools have formal swimming lessons, that a person who gets into difficulty in an aquatic environment takes note of the key to survival in swimming. This key is to conserve energy. The survival swimmer should consider the following guidelines:

- hold any buoyant object (anything that floats well)
- in cold water keep your clothing on
- keep yourself relaxed
- keep the body and limbs submerged
- swim with slow relaxed strokes
- change position and strokes often
- keep the eyes open
- breathe in a regular, controlled manner
- attract attention

The key to good swimming

It is important for the learner swimmer to stay *relaxed*. This will develop confidence and from this, mastery of water skills. It is also important to set goals for achievement, e.g. getting the face wet; completing a lap of freestyle. Whatever the level of achievement it must be considered as an individual's expectation and goal. Above all it is important to remember to swim for *fun*.

Buoyancy

Some people can float better than others and many factors can affect this. One important factor which can make a difference is the shape of the person. Are you fat, thin or muscular? A fatter person can usually float very easily particularly horizontally, on their back. A muscular person will have a much harder task trying to float.

Buoyancy is the result of the volume of water displaced. If a person displaces less water s/he will float higher in the water. Another factor that will affect this is the body position of the person. Different body positions will displace different amounts of water and improve an individual's ability to float. The amount of air in the lungs will also be an important factor. Fully inflated lungs can hold two to five litres of air and this provides greater buoyancy.

Finally, the type of water that the swimmer is in will affect buoyancy. Salt water has a slightly higher specific gravity and is easier for everyone to float in. Are you a 'sinker' or a 'floater'?

Hygiene

All swimmers should be aware of other people in an aquatic environment, and especially in a swimming pool. They should:

- not swim if they have any foot or skin infections
- not swim in their normal clothes. They should wear bathers or other type of costume
- where possible the toilet and showers should be used before entering the pool
- feet should be washed prior to entering the pool
- food, including chewing gum should be prohibited in and around the pool or other aquatic environment
- outdoor shoes should not be worn in or around the pool surroundings

WORK IT OUT!

Answer the following questions and write your answers in your exercise books. You will find the answers on page **156** at the back of this book.

1. In what year did swimming become an Olympic event?
2. What were the first swimming strokes to be developed?
3. Who was the man who developed the crawl-stroke?
4. In what country did the crawl-stroke develop?
5. What is the name of the stroke where the hands enter together above the water level and the feet kick downwards and together?
6. Name one survival swimming stroke.
7. What is the key to survival swimming?
8. Name one important consideration for the learner swimmer.
9. Who can float better on the back, a muscular person or a fat person?
10. If a person displaces less water will s/he float higher or lower in the water?

part three

Team Games

- *Softball*
- *Netball*
- *Soccer*
- *Touch*
- *Basketball*
- *Volleyball*
- *Cricket*
- *Hockey*

10 Softball

History

The game of softball developed from the game of baseball in the U.S.A. Baseball itself first developed from the game of cricket, which came from England.

Softball uses a larger ball than baseball. The pitcher's delivery is underarm in softball, while an overarm throw is used in baseball. Softball was first played in a factory warehouse in Chicago in 1887, as a way to fill in lunch hours. Made-up equipment was used, such as a boxing glove for a ball and a broomstick for a bat. In each local community the game had different rules and a different name. Some of these names included mush ball, pumpkin ball, diamond ball, kitten ball, and recreation ball.

In 1926, 'softball' became the sport's official name. Although the game is called 'softball', the ball is actually quite hard. In 1926, the rules also became standardised. Softball was spread to various parts of the world by American soldiers based in different countries during World War II. This is how softball was introduced to Papua New Guinea. The game today still remains most popular in the coastal and island regions where the soldiers were based.

Papua New Guinea first competed internationally in the 1965 Women's World Championships in Australia. Now both men's and women's teams compete internationally. Over seventy countries play the sport worldwide. Fast pitch women's softball was a medal sport for the first time at the Olympic Games in Atlanta in 1996.

Types of softball

Many different versions of the game exists. When classifying which version of the game, the position of pitcher is often important. As the name suggests, 'fast pitch softball' uses fast pitches to make batting and scoring runs difficult. The pitcher uses a windmill pitching action. The pitcher plays a very important part of the team and contributes up to seventy per cent of the fielding team's success.

'Slow pitch softball' was designed to promote batting. This type of softball is popular in the northern hemisphere. Pitchers use an underarm slingshot delivery which allows more successful hits, more runners on base, more team fielding, and higher scoring games.

Softball may be modified for younger players learning to play the game. It is called 't-bol' in the Pikinini Modified Sports programme. The emphasis is placed on participation, enjoyment and skill development, using modified rules and equipment. One of the major changes in t-bol is that the ball is hit off a batting stand shaped like a 'T' rather than using a specialised pitcher position.

The aim of the game

Each team consists of nine or sometimes ten players. If there are ten players in a team, the tenth player is called a 'designated batter'. A designated batter is a specialist batter who bats for the team but does not field. The aim of the game is to score more runs (running a complete circuit of the diamond) than the opposition. Each run scores one point. A home run is given when the batter hits the ball over the boundary on the full, or hits the ball within the boundary but runs past all bases including home base before the ball is returned to the catcher for a tag out.

The game is normally controlled by three umpires. The most important umpire is known as the 'plate umpire' and stands behind the catcher and judges the pitches, the hits and the outs at home plate.

Figure 10.1 The plate umpire stands behind the catcher

The two base umpires are positioned initially at first and third base, and change positions during the game according to where base runners are stationed. Base umpires call plays at first, second, and third bases, and assist the plate umpire.

The game lasts for either a designated time, for example, 1½ hours, or for a set number of innings, for example, seven. An innings means when both teams have batted and fielded. At the end of this period the runs are counted and the team with the most runs is the winner.

The playing field

Softball is played on an outdoor field called a softball diamond. The diamond is divided into two areas: an infield and an outfield. There are also two important areas known as 'fair' and 'foul' territory. Runs will only be scored if the ball is hit into fair territory. The softball field has many complicated markings, some of which are not necessary for Physical Education classes, but would be introduced at club level. The field size is reduced in two areas in women's softball. The pitching distance of 14.02 m in men's softball is reduced to 12.19 m, and the boundary fences of 68.58 m become 60.96 m. The distances between the bases, however, remain the same for both the men's and women's games.

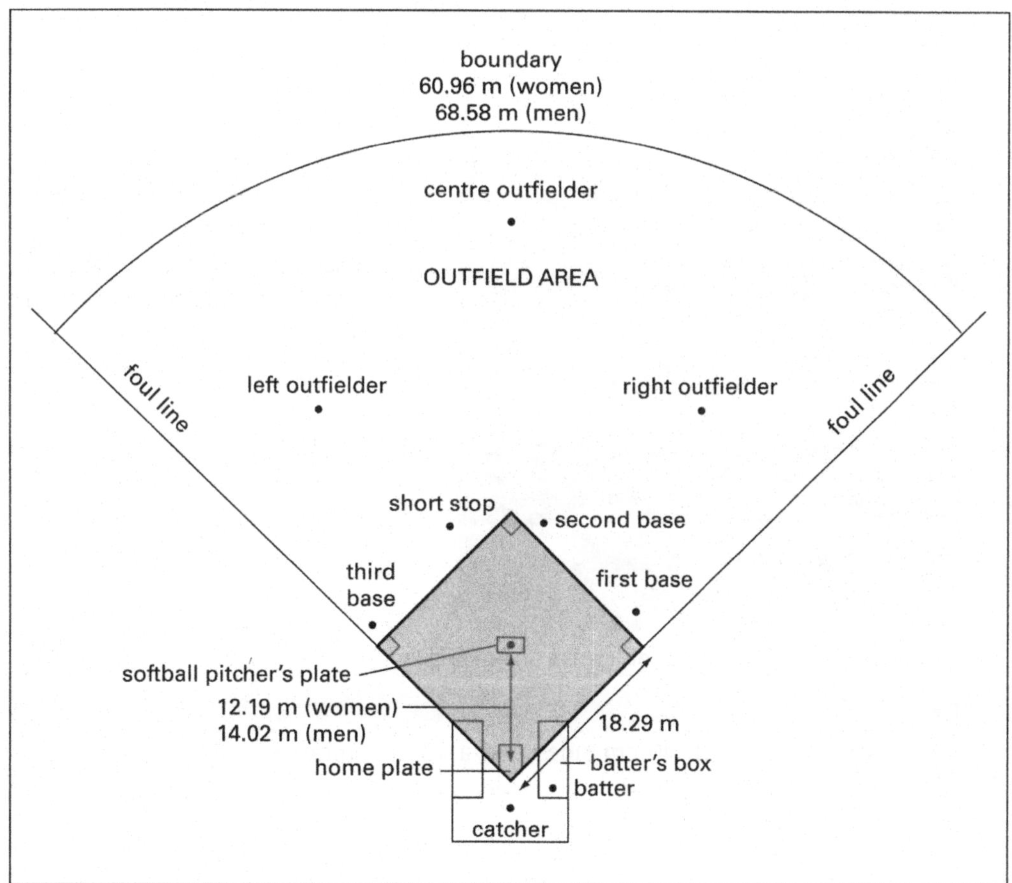

Figure 10.2 The softball diamond

Equipment

Softball is a sport that requires a large amount of equipment. It is a very exciting game, but players can get hurt if hit by a carelessly thrown or swung bat, or hit by the ball, when thrown or pitched quickly. The ball *is* hard and the bat *is* heavy. Therefore the equipment is necessary for safety measures.

The catcher's full protective gear includes a face mask, throat protector, chest protector, and shin guards. The bat, the ball, and catcher's equipment are essential. Improvised equipment can be used for bases, marking the lines, and so on but it is important that improvised equipment doesn't change the skill of the game. Sticks marking bases make it very difficult for players to learn how to run bases, slide, and tag out. Here is a list of the important equipment.

Ball

Rubber or leather with a diameter of 30.2 cm–30.8 cm

Bat

Wood, plastic, bamboo, graphite, metal, magnesium, or a combination of materials with a maximum length of 86.3 cm, and maximum weight of 1077.3 g

Figure 10.3 Players with the softball bat and gloves

Glove

Leather, and worn on the non-throwing hand (most gloves would be left-hand gloves for right handers). Catcher's and first base players are allowed special gloves with an enlarged pocket. It isn't necessary to put each finger in all the finger slots; try and leave the first slot free and put your index and middle finger in the second slot. This will give you a bigger catching space, and protect your fingers from injury.

Bases

Made from canvas with 40 cm sides and a 13 cm thickness (old mattresses cut into squares are a good substitute)

Homeplate

Diamond shaped and made of rubber or canvas. The diamond point faces the pitcher, and has measurements of 45 x 20 x 30 cm

Pitcher's plate

Wood, rubber, or canvas, and measures 60 x 15 cm

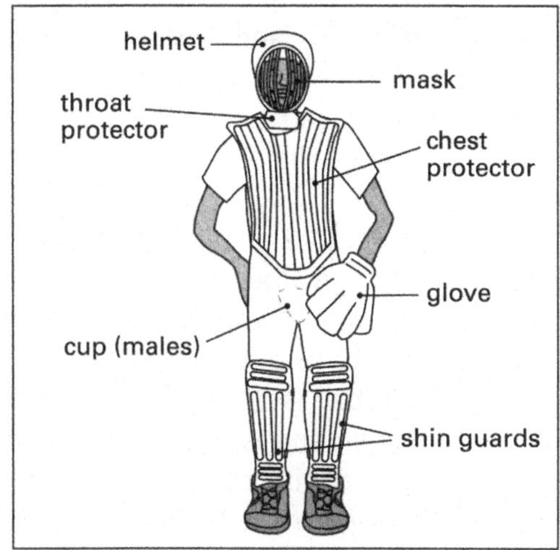

Figure 10.4 The catcher's full protective uniform

Catcher's equipment

The catcher's position can be dangerous, particularly being so close to a swinging bat! Extra equipment required for the catcher includes a face mask with throat protector to protect the face, mouth, and wind pipe. A chest protector prevents foul balls injuring the chest and internal organs. The shin guards protect the shins, knees, and ankles, which is especially important when blocking pitches, or fielding the ball when a baserunner tries to slide home.

Playing positions

The softball field is divided into an infield (the diamond) and the outfield. Each player has a specialised role known as their defensive position when fielding. All the fielding positions are within fair territory except the catcher, who stands behind homeplate.

Pitcher

The pitcher 'throws' the ball to the batter. Either an underarm release is used in the form of a windmill pitch (a full 360 degree rotation of the shoulder) or a slower slingshot pitch, which is truly underarm. A very skilled pitcher has a number of different pitches to choose from. These include fast, drop, rise, slow, and curve pitch. This makes it difficult for the batter to select which ball is fair to hit.

Figure 10.5 Pitching the ball

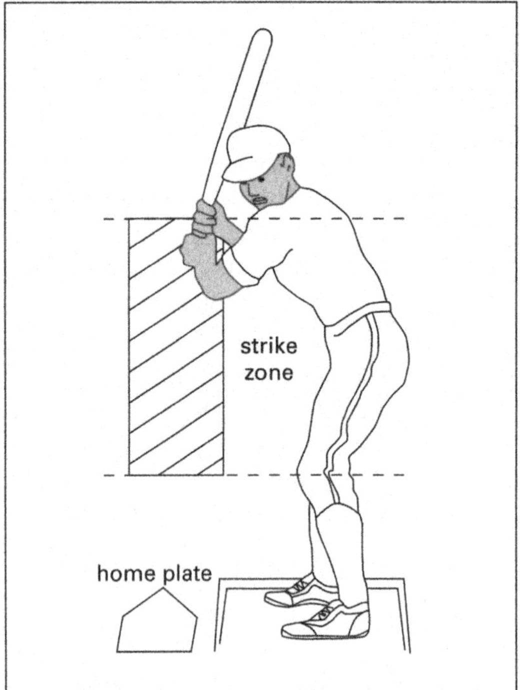

Figure 10.6 The strike zone

A 'strike' is a fair ball passing through the 'strike zone'. This is the area between the batter's knees and the sternum, and across home plate. A 'strike' is also called if the batter swings at a pitch which is not in the strike zone.

A 'ball' is a pitch that doesn't pass through the strike zone, nor is it swung at by the batter. Swinging at the ball turns a 'ball' into a 'strike' even if the ball is a long way away from the batter, and is impossible to hit. If the pitcher pitches four 'balls' the batter is allowed a free walk to first base. If the pitcher pitches a wild ball that hits the batter, a free walk is also given.

Figure 10.7 The batter is ready to strike

Catcher

The catcher is one of the most important defensive players in the team. The catcher's position is sometimes wrongly called the backstop. The backstop is actually the wire cage or netting behind the catcher which stops the ball after poor throws or loose pitches. The catcher squats behind the batter and catches or blocks the pitches not struck by the batter. S/he also calls the type of pitch to be delivered, using different hand signals. Fielding foul balls, short balls, throwing to infielders and, tagging out base runners trying to score runs crossing home base, are all the catcher's fielding duties. For this reason the catcher must be very agile.

First, second, third base players

These three positions are named after the base for which the fielder is responsible. Base players tag out runners trying to run to their base and also field balls close to their base area. The first base player must be able to catch hard, fast throws mainly from the infielders who are aiming to get the batter out running to first base. This is usually the first out option, and is known as the 'easy out'. Homebase is covered by the catcher.

Figure 10.8 Running for the base

Shortstop

The shortstop stands between third base and the pitcher in the infield, and is responsible for fielding balls around this area. They are usually very mobile players and have difficult balls to field, either hit into the ground with a difficult bounce (grounders) or flat and hard, with little time to react. The shortstop is mostly involved in the 'out on first' base play.

Outfielders

Outfielders are also named by their fielding positions and fielding areas. There are three outfield positions. Right outfield fields in the area behind and inwards from first base, centre outfield behind second base, and left outfield stands behind and inwards from third base. The positions are named from the catcher's viewpoint. The outfielders stand either close to the batter or out towards the boundary fence depending if the batter is a big hitter. Outfielders must be able to throw the ball a long way (remember that the boundary fences are over 60 m away), and be good at catching fly balls (above the head). A fielding hint for these players is that right hand batters usually hit to the left and centre outfield areas, while left hand batters hit to the right outfield area.

How to score runs: batting and bunting

There are two types of batting used in softball. One can be described as 'hitting out', which means hitting the pitch so the ball travels as far as possible or placing the ball amongst fielders to make fielding difficult.

Another type of batting is called 'bunting', when the ball is hit very softly and stops close to the batting box. A coach might ask a batter to bunt if the batter is a very fast runner, or to 'sacrifice' the batter's chance at making a base in order to advance baserunners. The last example is known as a 'sacrifice bunt'.

How to get a player out: fielding

There are many ways to get a player out in softball. They can be simply grouped as 'batting outs' or 'base running outs'. Batters must bat in a specific order that can't be changed after starting the game. Usually the best batters are at the start of the batting order, being more difficult to get out. Three 'outs' are needed before teams swap batting and fielding positions.

Ways to get a 'batter out'

- a fly ball hit into the air is caught on the full
- the ball is hit while one whole foot is outside the batting box or is touching homeplate
- after two strikes, the batter bunts a foul on the third strike
- a fair batted ball reaches first base before the batter does
- a batter leaves the bat on the base after running to first base
- a batter misses the third strike, which is caught by the catcher (this is known as a strike out).

Ways to get a 'base running out'

- a base runner is tagged running between bases
- a base runner is tagged while not touching a base
- a base runner runs on a fly ball that is successfully caught, and doesn't return to touch the previous base
- a forced-out is made, meaning the base runner must leave the base for another runner and the fielder has already tagged their base
- the base runner swerves outside the 0.9 m line when running between bases
- the base runner leaves the base before the ball has left the pitcher's hands
- the base runner interferes with a fielder attempting to field the ball.

HAVE A GO!

Here are some rules for playing a softball quiz. Divide into groups of five. One person in the team acts as the 'runner', collecting questions from the question bench and returning answers to the answer bench to be checked. If the answer given is correct, a tick is awarded to that team, and they collect the next question. If the answer is wrong the runner returns to the team to work out the correct answer. Each team can only progress to the next question if the correct answer is given. The first team to answer all the questions is the winner.

Organisation

Three students will be required to run the quiz. One is at the question bench, giving out questions. Another is the answer checker, and the third student is the scorer. Questions should be copied so that there are enough for each team, and cut into slips so that one question can be collected at a time. The answers for each question should be with the answer checker. The scorer can prepare a table on the blackboard with one column for teams and one column for questions correctly answered.

Here are some questions, but you will need to make up some more. The answers to the following questions are on page **156** at the back of this book.

1. Name two situations when a player can be given a walk.
2. When would a sacrifice bunt be used?
3. True or false? A player is out if s/he leaves the base before the ball leaves the pitcher's hand.
4. In the Pikinini Sport programme, what name is given to modified softball?
5. Who introduced softball to Papua New Guinea?
6. The softball diamond is another name for what area of the field?
7. What is the name of the outfielder position standing behind and inwards from first base?
8. Which umpire stands behind the catcher and calls the pitches?
9. A player who bats but does not field is known as what?
10. A batter who hits the ball over the boundary fence in fair territory is awarded what?
11. Name two ways a base runner can be given out.
12. True or false? Boundary fences, the pitching distance, and the distance between bases are all reduced in women's softball.

(Note: this quiz can be adapted to suit any sport.)

11 Netball

History

Netball developed from the game of basketball, although few similarities remain between the two sports today. In 1901 official rules for a more 'lady-like' form of basketball were devised in England. The game became known as Ladies Basketball, and was a non-contact sport. Ladies Basketball was introduced to different corners of the world by the British as they immigrated to other countries. Many rules were modified, e.g. the reduction of on-court players, from nine to seven-a-side; the playing areas were restricted. In 1970, netball emerged as the game we see played today.

Netball has become a popular women's sport, particularly in countries within Oceania. Leading netballing nations include Australia, New Zealand, South Africa, Trinidad and Tobago, Jamaica, and England. Although originally a sport for women, netball is now played by men in some countries. Mixed teams are popular in the modified game of indoor netball.

On the international scene, netball nations are invited to compete at the World Championships held every four years. In 1998, netball was introduced as an official sport at the Commonwealth Games.

The game of netball was introduced to Papua New Guinea by missionary women, and became popular in the coastal regions of Papua. In 1957, the first netball association was formed in Central Province where the game still remains very popular. The Papua New Guinea Netball Federation was established in 1962, and Papua New Guinea attended its first World Championships in New Zealand in 1975. Although netball has spread throughout the country the dominant areas are still Port Moresby, Lae, and Central Province.

The aim of the game

The aim of the game is for each team to score as many goals as possible in the time allowed. One point is awarded for each successful goal which must be scored from inside the goal circle. The game is usually played in two 20 minute halves for a total of 40 minutes, or in 15 minute quarters for an hour. The game starts from a centre pass-off in the middle of the court. Each team has alternative pass-offs from the centre so there is an equal chance for each team to score a goal.

The court

The court is divided into thirds: two goal thirds and the centre third with a goal post at each end. The playing surface can range from grass, wood, concrete, and sand. The important areas are the goal circles and the centre circle. Scoring goals is difficult in netball because the goal has no backboard like basketball. Goals must be scored from inside the goal circles. The game is started from the centre circle, and also recommences from there after each goal is scored. The ball cannot be thrown from one end of the court to the other, but must pass through each third of the court.

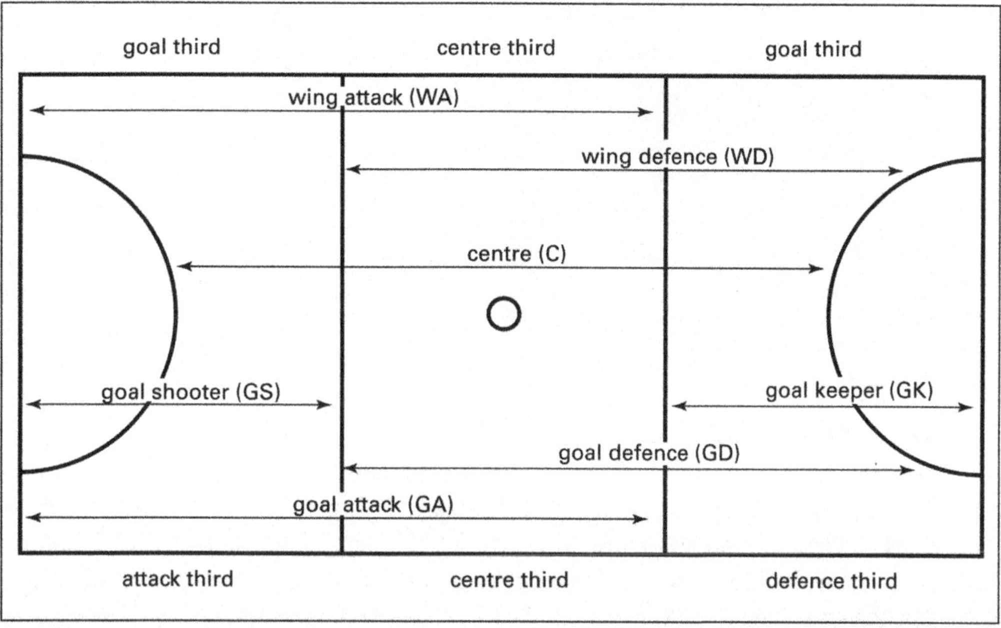

Figure 11.1 The netball court

Playing positions

In netball there are seven players from each team on court at one time. The team can total up to 12 players, including the reserves. Each player is only allowed in certain areas of the court, and has a specific job to do. Because of the limitations placed on the players by the court markings, netball playing positions are very specialised. The players wear bibs with the printed initials of their playing position. This is to make sure the umpire knows in which area of the court they are allowed to play. Some players such as the Centre cover most of the court and need to be very fit. Others like the Goal Keeper must be able to jump high to intercept passes and stop the opponents from scoring goals. Remember that, whether you are an attack or defence player, to be a good netballer, both strong attacking and defence skills are needed.

Goal Shooter (GS)

The Goal Shooter is an attacking player and plays in the goal third, including the goal circle. This player is usually the main shooter and should be able to score goals from anywhere in the goal circle.

Figure 11.2 Goal Attack shooting for goal

Goal Attack (GA)

The Goal Attack is the other player on court that is able to shoot goals. She is an important centre pass option and must have good passing skills to feed the Goal Shooter. This player has more court playing area, including the centre third, goal third, and goal circle.

Wing Attack (WA)

Another attacking player is the Wing Attack, who is usually a very fast player and needs to be able to change directions quickly. This player must be able to get free and pass the ball in many different ways to trick the defenders guarding the shooters. They receive most of the centre passes and can play within the centre and goal third, but not the goal circle.

Figure 11.3 The Centre receiving the ball

Centre (C)

The Centre player can play in all areas of the court except the goal circles. They have the job of being a linking player between the attack and defence players. The Centre is also responsible for the centre pass which means passing the ball from inside the centre circle when a goal has been scored.

Wing Defence (WD)

The main role of the Wing Defence is to restrict the movements of the Wing Attack so they have difficulty receiving passes. The wing defence plays in the same playing areas as the Wing Attack, which is the centre and goal third, excluding the shooting circle.

Figure 11.4 Goal Defence intercepting the ball

Goal Defence (GD)

The Goal Defence is one of the two defenders allowed in the goal circle to try to stop the opponents from scoring goals. The Goal Defence must have a good understanding with the Goal Keeper, the other circle defence player. The Goal Defence is usually very agile and can jump high to intercept shots and passes. This player is allowed in the centre third, goal third, and goal circle.

Goal Keeper (GK)

This player is sometimes thought of as the last line of defence and mostly defends within the goal circle. The Goal Keeper must be skilled at defending the shot and be able to rebound well, to clear the ball to the attacking end if the goal is missed. The Goal Keeper plays in the goal third and goal circle.

Skills of the game

Netball is a fast moving game with lots of different skills, making the sport exciting to watch. Netball players need to make quick decisions because the ball must be passed within three seconds. Players must not run with the ball, so different types of passing are used to move the ball quickly down court. The chest pass and one handed (or shoulder) pass are the most often used in netball. Other passes include the bounce pass and the overhead pass.

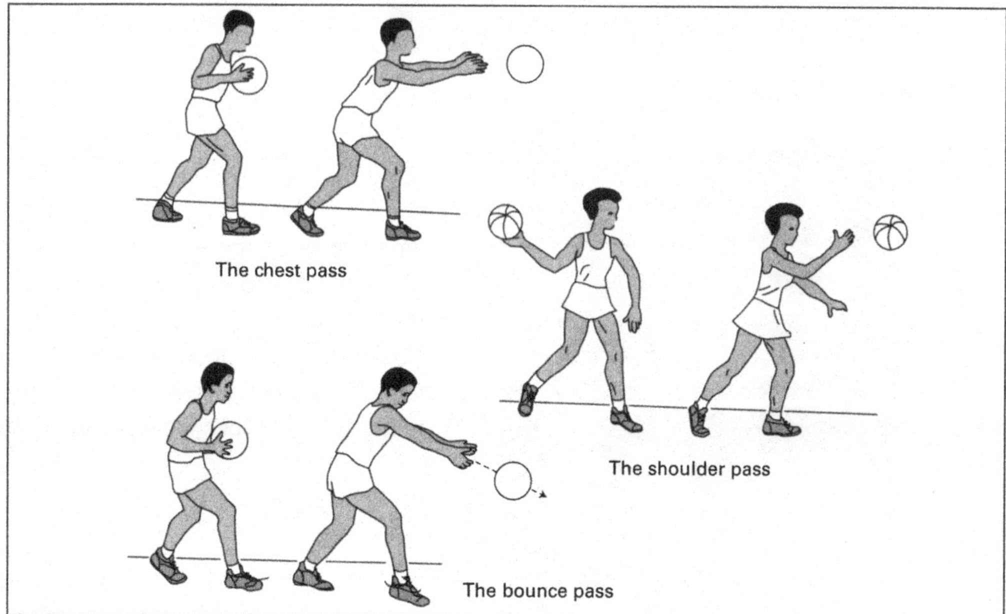

Figure 11.5 Chest pass, shoulder pass, bounce pass

Players get free from the defence players by using a variety of different movements. Good players are those that have a number of ways to get free. Some of these attacking moves are:

- dodging (pretending to go one direction, then running in the other)
- rolling (turning away from your player and running to the free space)
- sprinting
- sprinting using a change of direction.

Figure 11.6 Jumping to deflect the ball

Defending players usually use 'man to man' defence. This means the defender guards their partner. Defenders need to stay close to their partner and try to intercept the pass, or force an error. Circle defenders must practise leaning or jumping to deflect the ball or 'put the shooter off' while shooting.

Figure 11.7 Shooting for goal

Shooting accuracy is best developed using a one-handed shooting technique; the second hand provides support on the side of the ball. A balanced body position, a high release of the ball, and proper follow-through are important points to remember when shooting a goal.

Controlling the game

The game is controlled by two umpires. They umpire one half of the court each as well as the sidelines closest to them when the ball goes out of play. Umpires always control that part of the game that runs towards their right from half way. The umpire, whose end the last goal was scored, restarts play at the centre pass by blowing the whistle.

Basic rules

There are two basic distinctions when making rulings:

- serious errors are known as penalty passes
- less serious errors are called free passes

A penalty pass is awarded for contacts and obstructions. A 'contact' is when a player accidentally or intentionally bumps a player, or knocks the ball out of that player's hands. An 'obstruction' is also known as defending too close, which means the player is closer than 0.9 metres to the player with the ball. When an umpire calls a 'contact' or 'obstruction' the player that has made the mistake must stand alongside the thrower taking the penalty pass until the ball has left the thrower's hands.

Figure 11.8 Obstruction by Goal Defence

If the ball goes out of court a throw-in is taken by the other team where the ball left the court, by a player who must wait for the umpire to call 'play'. At those times where the umpire is not certain which team last touched the ball, a toss between two chosen players from each team is taken. A free pass is often awarded when an error has been made by the player with the ball.
Examples include:

stepping	the player has moved the grounded foot illegally
replayed ball	the player has controlled the ball, dropped it, and controlled it again
held ball	the player with the ball has failed to pass it in under three seconds
over a third	the ball has been thrown over a third of the court without being touched
offside	the player has stepped into a third of the court in which they are not permitted, as determined by their position.

WORK IT OUT!

Copy the following word puzzle into your exercise book and circle the netball terms in the word puzzle.

DODGE, STEPPING, WA, ROLLING, GOALPOST, THIRDS, OFFSIDE, CHESTPASS, BIB

C	H	D	O	D	G	E	S	X	T
H	Z	T	S	O	P	L	A	O	G
E	S	V	G	J	O	Y	B	F	D
S	R	T	I	U	H	R	M	F	N
T	K	H	E	L	D	O	C	S	Z
P	W	I	L	P	H	L	E	I	O
A	W	R	P	U	P	L	T	D	W
S	T	D	J	V	S	I	A	E	N
S	O	S	B	I	B	N	N	B	I
M	J	O	N	T	I	G	C	G	L

12 Soccer

History

It is uncertain exactly where and when soccer was first played. A kind of soccer called Tsu-Chi was played in China in the 3rd and 4th centuries B.C. In Europe the ancient Greeks developed a football type of game, like soccer. It is possible that the Romans introduced it to Great Britain. King Henry VII banned football in Great Britain because of the violence associated with it; he felt it was a game for hooligans. It was often the cause of misbehaviour, sometimes resulting in injury and death. Another reason was that the sport interfered with training in archery. This was a skill that was considered of more importance in time of war than the exercise obtained in playing football.

Football may have had its re-birth in a match played between the servants of the king and those of the English noblemen in 1681. The king gave his personal support and encouragement to the match.

English public schools gave the first set of rules to football, and in 1863 set up the football association to control the game. FIFA was formed in Paris in 1904. Football was played for the first time in the Olympics in 1908. The World Cup competition began in 1930 to permit professional football players also to participate, since the Olympics used to allow only amateurs to compete. The winner of the first World Cup was Uruguay, who defeated Argentina.

Mostly known as soccer here, it is very popular in Papua New Guinea. It is played in more regions of the country than rugby. There are competitions for women as well as men, and there are under age (youth) competitions as well. Papua New Guinea has both men's and women's international teams. They perform very well in regional tournaments against other South Pacific nations.

Soccer around the world

Soccer is one of the world's most popular games. More of the world's youth play soccer than any other sport. It is a different sort of game from most of the other popular team games, because the ball is played mostly with the feet and head rather than with the hands. Other parts of the body may be used to control or propel the soccer ball, but only the goalkeeper is permitted to touch the ball with the hands. The name 'soccer' comes from a short form of the term, 'Association Football'. The name 'football' can be misleading in different countries, e.g.

- When an American speaks of football, American football is what is usually meant (sometimes called 'gridiron').
- A New Zealander will probably be referring to Rugby Union.
- Ireland has its own national game of Gaelic football.
- Australia has its own Australian Rules football.

All these codes developed from the same basic game of football (soccer). The International Association Football Federation (FIFA), the organisation that governs football around the world, still uses the name 'football'. Over 175 countries, including Papua New Guinea, are members of FIFA.

Values of the game

One of the main objectives of soccer is to provide good recreation. It is a great way of keeping fit. The game requires a great deal of running, jumping, twisting and turning from all the players. General fitness and a high level of endurance, coordination, balance, speed, confidence, courage, quick thinking, initiative, and agility are developed through the game. Above all, it is fun!

Acquiring skills always gives satisfaction, and there is a lot of opportunity in soccer for anyone to learn new skills and to improve old ones. The very purpose of the game is ball control—stopping it, moving along with it, and then passing or kicking it. These skills are learned through hard practice and give much satisfaction and confidence.

Soccer is a team sport. A soccer player is a member of a group, playing with and being dependent upon the other team members. Each is helping the other, and selfishness has no part. Certainly there is place for each player to be an individual. Soccer would indeed be sad without its individuals. Further, this game can help in the successful development of an individual's personality and character.

Figure 12.1 The Korobosea under-8 champions 1993

Soccer is more than a simple game—it is an emotional experience. Somewhere in these emotions lies the key to 'the spirit of the game', a term often mentioned but not often defined. A close look at the thinking behind the laws provides three important clues to the interpretation of 'the spirit of the game'. First, all players must have an equal opportunity to demonstrate individual skills without undue interference from opponents. Physical size is not an essential requirement for success. Second, in normal match-play, the safety of each player is most important. Care is taken to remove anything which may prove dangerous. Third, the laws are specific on punishment of infringements and misconduct. The game is intended to be played within a code of conduct based on accepted principles of mutual respect between people for maximum enjoyment.

The playing field

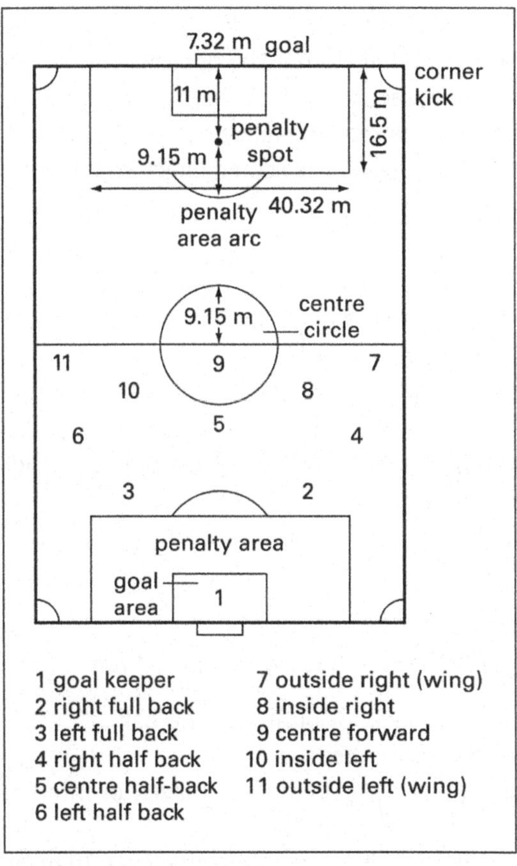

Figure 12.2 The field layout

Soccer is a game in which a team of eleven players try to get a round, inflated ball towards and between an opponent's goalposts and under its crossbar by dribbling, kicking, striking or pushing the ball with any part of the body except the arms and hands. The goalkeeper is the only player allowed to handle the ball.

Main rules of the game

The game is played by two teams of eleven players each. They are the:

- goalkeeper
- defenders

- midfield players
- forwards

According to the rules of the particular competition, there may be between one and three reserve players, as well as a reserve goalkeeper. However, once a player has been replaced, that player may not return to the game. A player sent from the game by the referee for a 'red card' offence may not be replaced.

The ball

The game is played with a round ball with a circumference of 68 cm–71 cm.

Start and resumption of play

The ball is put in play by a place kick taken from the centre of the field at the start of the game, at the start of the second half, and after each goal. After a goal is scored the team scored against, kicks the ball. Opposing players must stand at least 9.15 m away at the time of the kick. A goal cannot be scored direct from a kick off. The kicker cannot play the ball again until it has been played by another player. The opponents of the team that kicks off in the first half, kick off in the second half. When re-starting play after a temporary suspension of play, except on a free kick, the referee drops the ball at the place where it was when play was suspended. A goal may be scored direct from a dropped ball.

Players' privileges

Each player may control or gain possession of the ball in the following ways.

- A player may dribble, head the ball, or stop the ball by blocking it with any part of the body except the hands or arms.
- A player in possession of the ball may place him/herself between the opponent and the ball.
- A player may stop the ball by trapping it under the feet, between the feet, or between the front of the legs and the ground.
- A player may kick the ball while it is trapped by an opponent providing s/he does not commit a foul.

Playing privileges for the goalkeeper

A goalkeeper, within the penalty area, has the following additional privileges.

- S/he may pick up, bounce, throw, drop kick, or punt kick the ball.
- The ball may not be carried more than four steps.
- The goalkeeper may not be charged intentionally by any player, or interfered with, while in the goal area.
- Outside the penalty area, the goalkeeper has no more privileges than any other player.
- S/he may not handle the ball passed back by a team mate (unless it has been headed back).

Scoring

A goal is scored when the whole of the ball has passed over the goal line, between the goal posts and under the cross bar, as long as no infringement has previously occurred.

Throw in

A ball that goes out of bounds over the side lines is thrown in by a player on the side that didn't touch it last. The ball must be thrown in with both hands from behind and over the head. The thrower must face the field of play, and as the ball is released part of each foot must be in contact with the ground on or behind the side line.

Goal kick

This is awarded to the defending team when the ball goes over the goal line, having last been touched by an attacking player. The ball is placed in any half of the goal area and the kicker must send the ball out of the penalty area. The kicker may not touch it again until another player has touched it. All other players must be outside the penalty area. A goal may not be scored direct from a goal kick.

Corner kick

This is awarded to the attacking team if the ball goes over the goal line having last been touched by a defender. The kick is taken from the quarter circle in the corner of the side where the ball went out. All opponents must remain 9.15 m away from the kicker. A goal may be scored direct from a corner kick, but the kicker may not kick the ball again until another player has played the ball.

Free kick

When a free kick is taken it must be played from the place where the infringement occurred. The ball may be kicked in any direction. Players of the opposite team must be 9.15 m away from the ball until the free kick is taken. There are different types of free kicks as follows:

1. Direct free kick

A direct free kick is given if a player commits any of the following offences:

- kicks or tries to kick an opponent
- trips an opponent
- charges into an opponent in a violent or dangerous way
- charges into an opponent from behind, unless the opponent was obstructing
- strikes (hits) or attempts to strike or spit at an opponent
- holds an opponent
- pushes an opponent with his hand or any part of his body
- handles the ball intentionally

A goal can be scored from a direct free kick.

2. Indirect free kick

An indirect free kick is given if a player:

- plays dangerously
- charges or obstructs an opponent without intending to play the ball
- attempts to play the ball when it is in possession of the goalie

- touches the ball a second time before another player touches it after a free kick, throw in, corner kick or penalty kick
- the goal keeper carries the ball more than four steps
- is in an offside position.

A goal cannot be scored straight from an indirect free kick. At least two people must touch the ball before a goal can be scored.

3. Penalty kick

A penalty kick is awarded if any of the rules for a direct free kick are broken in a defender's own penalty area. This free kick is taken from the penalty spot. All players except the goal keeper and the player taking the kick must stand outside the penalty area, at least 9.15 metres from the penalty spot. The goal keeper must stand on the goal line without moving his/her feet until the ball has been kicked. The kicker may not kick the ball twice. After the kick it must be touched by another player before s/he may play it again.

Offside

A player is offside when s/he is nearer the opponent's goal line than the ball at the moment the ball is played, unless:

- s/he is in his/her own half of the field
- there are two opponents nearer to their own goal line than s/he is
- s/he receives the ball direct from a goal kick, corner kick, a throw-in, or it has been dropped by the referee.

A player cannot be offside:

- if s/he is behind the ball when it is played by a team member
- if two opponents are between him/her and the goal when the ball is next played by a team member.

Note: Even if an opponent is in line with him/her, it is considered as having two opponents between him/her and the goal.

HAVE A GO!

HAVE A GO!

Here are some skills for you to practise. The more you practise the better you will become.

Cushioning the ball

Kick the ball gently, and try to keep the ball cushioned against your leg. Try it with your chest and thighs.

Juggling the ball

This helps you practise your ball control and is fun to try. Keep the ball in the air for as long as possible using your feet, thigh, chest, or head.

- Practise on your own: Juggle using only your feet, head, or thigh. Juggle using different parts of your foot, e.g. inside of foot, outside of foot, shoe laces.

- Practise with a partner: Have a competition to see which person can juggle the longest. In groups of 4 or 6 see which group can keep the ball in the air for the longest period.

Figure 12.3 Juggling with the ball

Running with the ball

Running with the ball is not the same as dribbling. Dribbling means dodging players. Running with the ball means moving the ball quickly when there are no defenders.

- Practise on your own: Run with the ball from the goal line to half way using the inside and outside of your foot. Run with the ball to a marker, dodge quickly to the side, then go to the next marker, and so on.
- Practise with a partner: Race over set distances, running with the ball.

Figure 12.4 Running with the ball using the inside and outside of the foot

Dribbling

This means running past defenders while keeping the ball under control. You have to be able to change pace, change direction, feint (*pretend* to change direction), and create space to allow you to pass or perhaps shoot at goal.

- Practise on your own: Dribble around a small marked out area. Use the inside and outside of your foot to control the ball. Stop the ball using the bottom of your foot. Dribble one way and change direction quickly. Try to trick your opponent.
- Practise with a partner: Play a one-on-one game in a small area, e.g. 20 m x 10 m. Get the ball to your opponent's goal line by dribbling past him/her.

Figure 12.5 Dribbling by stepping over the ball, on the ball, and by pulling the ball back

Kicking the ball

1. The *push pass* is the most reliable pass over a short distance. Use the inside of your foot.

Figure 12.6 Kicking using the inside of the foot

- Practise on your own: Kick the ball against a wall about five metres away and see how many passes you can complete without losing control. Use both feet.
- Practise with a partner: One person is the goalkeeper. The other shoots from about 10 m or 12 m to the goal with the inside of the foot.
- Kick with the outside of the foot. Flick the ball with the outside of your foot; kick through the middle of the ball. The action is disguised more when passed with the outside of the foot, and your running is not interrupted.

Figure 12.7 Kicking with the outside of the foot

Figure 12.8 Kicking with the instep

2. The *low drive* is kicked with the instep of your shoe (the laces). It takes a lot of practice to get this shot correct every time.

- Take an angled approach to the ball, put your non-kicking foot alongside the ball pointing in the direction you want the ball to go, and kick through the horizontal mid-line of the ball.
- Practise with a partner: Kick low drives to each other across an area about 10 m by 20 m. Have a penalty shoot-out. Kick ten each from the penalty spot.

3. The *lofted pass* is a long kick to get the ball over defenders. Approach the ball from a slight angle, and the non-striking foot should be behind and to the side of the ball. Keep the ankle of your kicking foot firm, and strike the ball below the mid-line with the lace of the shoe.

- Practise with a partner: Practise the lofted pass in an area of about 10 m x 40 m. Score a point if you land it close to your partner.

4. The *volley* is kicked when the ball is in the air. When volleying kick the ball with your instep lace. Kick through its mid-line, keeping your toe down. Sometimes the ball comes from the side, and you have to adjust by leaning away from the ball. This is the side volley or pivot volley.

5. The *half-volley* is when you kick the ball just as it touches the ground. Like ordinary volleying, the half-volley is used in both attack and defence.

Figure 12.9 Kicking a half volley

Receiving the ball

You must be able to control the ball quickly when it is passed to you in a game, and immediately decide what to do next.

- Practise on your own: Throw the ball in the air and control it with the bottom of your shoe. This is called 'wedge' control. Now control the ball as it hits the ground. Use the inside and outside of your foot, and move away with the ball.

Heading

Heading the ball is not difficult if you perform it correctly. A header can be used as a pass, a shot, or to clear the ball when defending. Remember, when heading use your upper forehead to strike the ball, not the top of your head, and do not let the ball hit you. Move your head towards the ball with the upper half of your body, then head through the ball.

- Practise on your own: See how many headers you can do by juggling. Use a wall and see how many headers you can do against it.
- Practise as a group: Play 'head tennis'. Keep the ball in the air as long as possible. Try heading the ball over a volleyball net.

Goal keeping

Stand with your feet shoulder-width apart, your body weight forward, and your arms slightly outside the line of your body. Keep your eyes on the ball. The word 'cup' is often used here. It means to hold your hands open and just a little apart, palm outwards and your fingers pointing down. As the ball arrives, bring your hands and arms under and around the ball, so that it is held very tightly into your body and cannot bounce out.

1. *Ground shots*: there are two basic ways of stopping a ground shot. To use the stoop method: get behind the ball, feet close together. Stoop from the waist and cup the ball into your arms. To use the kneeling method: get behind the ball. Drop onto one knee (it should almost touch the opposite foot). Turn at right angles to the ball. Cup the ball into your arms.

2. *Waist high shots*: get your body behind the ball and cup it into your waist.

3. *Chest high shots*: to get this ball, you may have to jump slightly. Otherwise, use the same technique as for the waist high ball.

4. *Head high shots*: catch the ball with your hands in a 'W' shape. Relax your fingers to take the speed of the ball. Punch the ball away only when you cannot catch it. This will usually be when you are surrounded by players.

Range of vision

Most young players play with their heads down, not often watching what is happening around them. Keeping an eye on the movement of other players encourages and supports a decision about what to do with the ball, and where to run, before the ball is even received. As players improve their skill and control, they learn to glance away from the ball to check possibilities for passing, shooting, and so on, while the ball still is in flight. Don't watch the ball for the whole of its movement towards you.

Speed of decision

Soccer is very much a game of decision. It is certainly important that the decision should be correct. Soccer educates players to think quickly and make early decisions. Learn and practise as much as you can, to enjoy the excitement of playing this fascinating game.

13 Touch

Introduction

Touch is a sport that is gaining increasing popularity around Melanesia and around the world. This is especially true in countries which have a strong history of rugby league or rugby union. Touch is an excellent game because it combines the major elements of rugby, but removes the tackling, scrums, and hard kicking. There are no goal posts. This makes it popular with parents and schools because the risk of injury is greatly reduced. Yet the skills and strategies of the game, such as running speed, agility, and ball handling, are all retained. This makes the game suitable for girls and women as well as men. Indeed, it makes the game available for mixed teams to play, with no additional problems. Women handle the game as well as men, and can compete or cooperate effectively with them when playing touch.

Figure 13.1 Women playing a game of touch in Port Moresby

The aim of the game

The aim of touch is to move the ball towards the opponents' scoreline by running and passing the ball backwards to team-mates. A goal is scored when the ball is placed on the ground over the goal-line. It is called a touchdown. Each team is given six chances to score, by keeping possession for six touches. After six touches, the ball is passed over to the opposing side and play restarted with a tap. Touch is usually played between two teams of seven players. In school there may be two teams of six to eleven players.

The playing field

The field is a simple rectangle with a halfway line. It should measure about 50 m x 35 m.

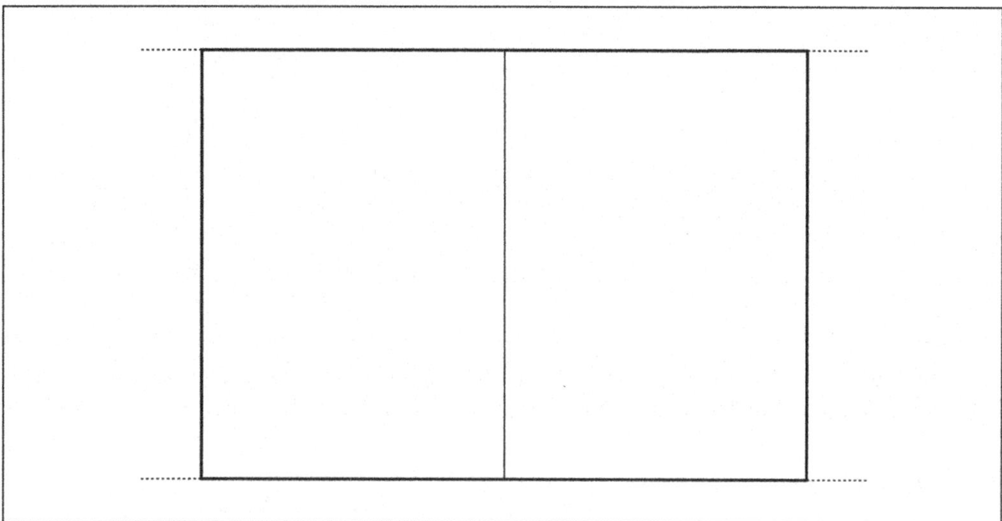

Figure 13.2 The playing area

Equipment

The ball should be the size of a junior rugby union ball, no larger. When practising, any type of football, soccerball, or netball could be used. Footwear that will not slip on the grass or ground is recommended.

How to play

Here are some important touch definitions.

Tap

This is the method of starting or restarting the game. The ball is placed on the ground, tapped slightly forward with one foot and picked up again. The forward tap is no more than one metre.

Touch

A defender touches either the holder of the ball or the ball itself.

Play-the-ball or Roll-ball

This is how the ball is brought into play following a touch. The touched player stands at the position of the touch and rolls or pushes the ball backwards on the ground between the legs towards the acting-half. The pass should be no longer than one metre.

Acting-half

The player behind the player who is playing-the-ball.

Marker

The defender who may stand in front of the opposition player playing-the-ball.

Touchdown

The scoring action of placing the ball on the ground past the goal-line or on it.

On-side

All team members must be between the ball and their own goal-line.

Offside

When a player is between the ball and the opposition goal-line.

Substitution

Can occur at any time. The player must leave the field before the substitute moves on.

Quarter

The game lasts for four quarters, from ten to fifteen minutes each quarter. There is a five minute break after the second quarter. Ends are changed after each quarter.

Rules

The team players are as follows:

- two wingers
- two links
- two or three middles

Start of play

Begins with a tap by the team who wins the toss. The defenders, except for the marker, must be back ten metres from the leading attackers at all taps. The referee usually stands at a position which shows where the ten metres distance is. The defenders use the referee's position and call as a guide where to line up to defend against the attackers.

Dropped ball

If the attacking team drops the ball, play is stopped, and the ball is handed (or turned) over to the opposition. Play is restarted by the referee saying, 'Play-the-ball'.

Touched player

A player who is touched by an opponent must stop, return to where s/he was touched, and play the ball.

Failure to stop

A penalty is awarded if the touched player does not stop. The defenders take possession and restart with a tap.

Figure 13.3 Touching an opponent

Play-the-ball

At play-the-ball, all defenders except the acting-half must be five metres behind the touch point and must not move until the acting-half has the ball. Again, the referee usually stands at a point about five metres behind the ball, which is a guide to the defenders where to line up across the field, ready for the 'play-the-ball'.

Acting-half

The acting-half may run with the ball, but if touched, possession is turned over to the defenders.

Forward passing

There is no forward passing. All ball passing must be backwards. Infringements result in a penalty with a tap re-start to the opposition.

Figure 13.4 Looking to pass the ball backwards

Out of play

Play is re-started by the opposition using play-the-ball if the ball goes out of the field.

Onside

All players must be onside during a play-the-ball.

HAVE A GO!

Practise these skills to improve your game.

1. Mark out a grid of squares with sides ten metres long. To start have three people in each square so there needs to be enough squares in the grid for everybody. Move around inside the square, passing the ball to each other. Keep the ball moving.

Figure 13.5 Passing the ball in threes

2. While on the run, try passing the ball just in front of the receiver, but behind the passer, so that the player can keep running without changing stride.
3. Practise the acting-half pass. Watch the ball. Place both hands on the ball and gently swing it from the ground straight to the receiver. Signal to the team by putting the left foot forward for a pass to the right and the right foot forward for a pass to the left.

Figure 13.6 A pass to the right

4. Two or three pairs race against the other pair(s) while passing the ball on the run. Run the length of the field while passing, then return. This makes sure that each pair passes to both left and right sides.

5. Practise play-the-ball. During a play-the-ball or tap, each defender should very quickly line up opposite an attacker, to mark them very closely.

6. Practise tapping the ball.

7. Practise team passing in lines, moving slowly forward, but passing the ball slightly behind. Increase the speed of the whole team, both while running forward and with the speed of the passing. As soon as the ball has reached the player at the end of the line, in order to keep the passing under way, the player in possession must sprint forward to get into a position to be able to pass the ball backwards across the line.

Figure 13.7 Passing in a line

8. Practise accelerating (quickly speeding up) and decelerating (slowing down).

9. Practise passing at the catcher's hands. Always look to where you are passing the ball. When passing start with the outside foot forward.

10. Spend as much spare time as possible practising quick passes which make the defenders lose sight of the ball, or lose their balance because of the quick change of direction.

Figure 13.8 A defender losing balance

Some excellent passes to try are:

- long passes, to an unmarked winger who can gain a lot of ground down the wing
- short passes, only a little flick upwards, to a player running quickly across behind you, to change the direction of play.

11. Practise making the touch, also known as 'effecting the touch'.
Points to watch as a defender making the touch: look at the waist/lower trunk of the attacker. Slow down a little bit, lean forward with the arm bent a little, and hand ready to make the touch. Avoid body-to-body contact. As an attacker with the ball, it can often be useful to keep a continuing attacking move under way by holding the ball or an arm forward to be touched by the defender.

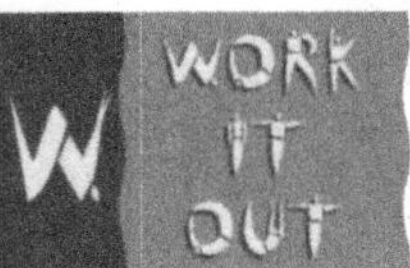

WORK IT OUT!

Answer these questions together in your groups.
1. What are two main differences between touch and rugby?
2. What is the main aim of the game?
3. What is the main method of play?
4. How many chances is the team in possession given to score?
5. How is the game restarted after a penalty has been awarded?
6. How far back must the nearest defender be from the player tapping the ball?
7. The player receiving the return pass on a play-the-ball is called __________ .

Now go out and play the game. It's fun!

14 Basketball

History

In 1891 in the United States, a Physical Education teacher named James Naismith decided he needed to improve the college football team's fitness. This was during winter when it was too cold to train outside because of the snow and cold temperatures. He thought of an indoor game which could be played in the school's gymnasium. This game involved two teams and used a soccer ball. Each team could bounce and pass the ball to avoid the opposition gaining possession. The aim of the game was to score as many goals as possible by throwing the ball through a woven peach-basket nailed on the wall at either end of the gymnasium. This aim is still the same today for the 100 year old sport—to score as many points as possible while trying to restrict the other team or opposition from scoring. The team which does this job the best is the winner.

From its simple beginning, basketball has become a very popular sport, and is played in over 175 countries in the world, including Papua New Guinea. It is a fast and exciting game, which is played by both men and women. The United States is very powerful in the sport because of its professional competitions and history of successes, e.g. the amazing 'Dream Team'.

How to play

Basketball is played on a court which can use a concrete, wooden, grass or clay surface. The basketball is a size five rubber ball for the adult game while mini basketballs are used for the modified children's game.

The game is started with a 'jump ball' between opposing players at the centre circle of the playing area. The ball is then passed or dribbled to each team's offensive (attacking) basket to attempt to score goals through the hoop or basket. Behind the basket is a backboard which can be used for the ball to bounce against, or go 'in off' to score a goal. Different points are given to different successful shots. This depends on how far the shooter was away from the basket when scoring and if any errors have been made or rules of the game broken.

Successful shots at the basket are worth two points for a field goal, three points for a field goal made outside the designated three point line, and one point for a free throw. The team with the most points at the end of the game wins.

The game is played for 40 minutes, divided into two 20 minute halves. Each coach is also allowed to call 'time-outs'. These signal a break in play where the coach can give further instructions to the players on court.

Figure 14.1 Shooting for a basket

The court

The markings on the court are:

- out of court boundaries, where throw-ins are taken
- the centre line which divides the court into two halves, and over which the ball cannot be passed back
- the centre circle, where the game commences
- the free throw line
- the three point line shows players from where to attempt their shots
- the key, close to the basket, where the defensive team can spend unlimited time, but the offensive players must move in and out, spending no more than three seconds inside.

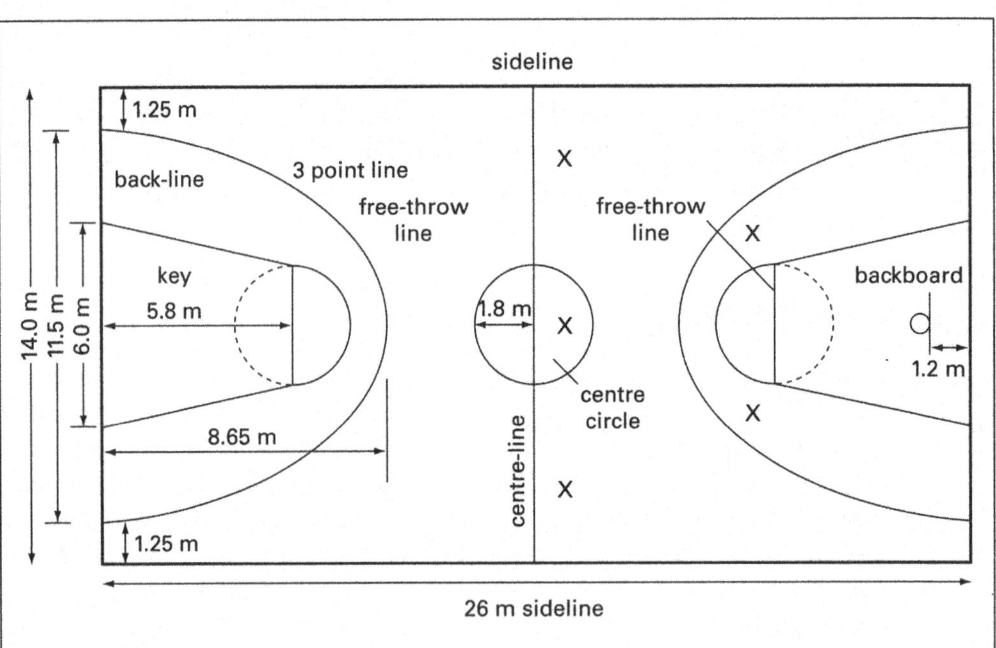

Figure 14.2 Basketball court markings and dimensions

The players

The entire team has ten players, but only five players may be on the court at any one time. The other five are substitutes or bench players. These players can be substituted for court players at any time during the game when there is a time-out or a jump ball (when play has stopped for a foul, or in some cases when the ball has gone out of bounds). The coach calls a 'substitution' and notifies the officials' bench which player will be replaced and which player will take the court. Substitutions are made for skill reasons, fitness reasons, or to avoid being 'fouled out of the game'. This is explained later.

The five court positions are:

- two guards, who have a big defensive responsibility
- two forwards, who are usually accurate shooters
- a centre, who links both ends of the court and is probably very speedy with great ball skills

One of the advantages of basketball is that all players have the opportunity to play offence, e.g. pass, dribble, and shoot baskets; and play defence, e.g. defend the player and the ball, and go for rebounds on the shot.

The rules

These are judged by the two referees who control the game. Basketball is a non-contact sport, but sometimes the game can become quite physical, especially in a tight contest. There are many rules the players must learn in order to play the game safely and skilfully. Following are some of the most important rules.

Dribbling

If a player wants to move the ball this can be done by dribbling, which is bouncing the ball with one hand. Dribbling is not allowed with both hands (which is what small children do), nor is it permissable to dribble, catch the ball, then dribble again. This is called a 'double dribble'.

Figure 14.3 Dribbling with the ball

Three second rule

When a team has the ball in offence, a player cannot stay in the key for more than three seconds. If this happens the opposition takes a throw-in from the side line.

Five second rule

A closely guarded player who is holding the ball must pass, shoot, or dribble the ball within five seconds; if not, the opposition takes a throw-in.

Ball returned to back court

The team with the ball in the front court can't pass to a player in the back court. If this error is made, a throw-in is taken by the other team.

Held ball

A 'held ball' occurs when a player from each team has hands firmly on the ball. The referee tosses the ball high, and a jump for the ball decides possession.

Figure 14.4 Jump for the ball

Personal foul

This is a player foul, which involves contact with a player on the opposite team. A personal foul could be awarded for a block, hold, push, charge, or trip. If the foul is committed when the player isn't shooting, a throw-in is awarded. If the fouled player was shooting and the attempted shot didn't go in, two free throws are awarded. If the shot is successful, two points are scored and one free throw is taken.

Figure 14.5 The defending player commits a foul

Five fouls by a player

If any player receives five fouls in the game they must automatically leave the game. They can be replaced by a substitute.

The skills

To be able to play basketball well, you need to practise your skills. Basketball skills can be practised by the team and by yourself in your spare time. A good basketballer is able to control the ball. There are lots of activities you can use to practise ball handling, dribbling, and passing skills.

HAVE A GO!

Give some of the next activities a try and improve your basketball skills!

Ball Handling

1. Ball wrap

Pass the ball from hand to hand, moving it around your body. Move the ball from your head to your feet and back again. How fast can you go without losing control of the ball?

2. Finger walk

Using your finger tips only, roll the ball down one side of your body and up again, keeping control with just your finger tips. Try with the other hand.

3. Figure-eight wrap

Stand with your legs apart, moving the ball through and around legs in the shape of a figure-eight. Make sure you don't drop the ball. To make it harder, keep your head up so you're not watching the ball as you move it around. Now try walking backwards and forwards. Because your back is bent all the time, this can be really exhausting!

Figure 14.6 Fast hands

4. Fast hands

Keep your legs apart and hold the ball with both hands (one at the front, one at the back) between your legs. Use fast hands and change their position on the ball before the ball lands on the ground. To start with, you can let the ball go upwards when you release it to allow more time to react.

5. Over-Under

Hold the ball with two hands in front of your body, then pass it just over your head. Quickly bring your hands to the back to catch the ball, then open your legs wide and bounce the ball through to the front. Repeat this, then work through from the back, bounce through to the front.

Dribbling

1. Stationary dribble

Dribble with both your left and right hand. Keep the dribble going and kneel down, sit down, and lastly lie down. Can you still keep the dribble going? Now rise from the floor to sitting, to kneeling, and back on to your feet.

Figure 14.7 Stationary dribble

2. Figure-eight Dribble
Place two markers or cones on the ground and dribble around the cones making a Figure-eight pattern. Change hands and continue. See how fast you can run and dribble without losing control of the ball.
3. Obstacle course dribble
Mark out an obstacle course with markers or cones. Dribble through the course forwards, then go through the course backwards. Time yourself and see if you can beat your best time.
4. Underneath dribble
As you are walking and dribbling, bounce the ball through your legs as you step forward. If you are using your right hand, push the ball through as you step forward with your left foot. If you are using your left hand, push the ball through as you step forward onto your right foot.
5. Here-there-where dribble
If you are practising with a friend, you can play here-there-where dribble. Your friend points to a spot on the court and you must dribble as quickly as possible to that area. When you get there your friend points to another place and you move there. This activity is a good way to practise dribbling with your eyes watching someone else.

Passing

It is important to catch and pass well in basketball and protect the ball from opponents who might steal the ball out of your hands. For these activities you'll need the help of your team mates.
1. Catch-pull
Your partner holds the ball above your head. You kneel down on the ground and, reaching up with both hands, pull the ball out of your partner's hands and in close to your chest. Try this about ten times, then let your partner have a turn.

2. Passing into space

Stand far enough apart from your partner to pass a chest pass. Pass two passes, then run around your partner and back to your place. As you are running back, your partner passes you the ball. Pass two more passes, then your partner runs around. Continue until you both need a rest.

Figure 14.8 Different passes to practise

Figure 14.9 Set shot, lay-up shot, hook shot

3. Variety passing

For this activity you need five players or more. Variety passing lets you practise all the different types of passing you might need to use in the game. Standing in a square, **A** passes a chest pass diagonally to **B**. **B** uses a bounce pass to **C**, **C** passes a one-handed javelin pass to **D**, and **D** passes an overhead pass to **E**. After your pass you run around the outside of the square to where you passed the ball.

Shooting

There are four different types of shots in basketball: set shot, lay-up shot, hook shot, jump shot. The easiest two are the set shot and lay-up, so practise these first.

1. Spot Shooting

Mark different spots around the basket and practise shooting from each of them. How many shots can you make without missing?

2. One-on-one

With a friend (as opponent), practise both dribbling and shooting, one-on-one. From the centre line dribble the ball so you are within range of the basket. Depending on your opponent's defence, go in for a lay-up or play a set shot. If you are successful with your shot, your partner plays the ball in from the centre line. If your shot misses, and your opponent gets the rebound, the ball must be played out to the centre line before attempting a shot.

Figure 14.10 Practising one-on-one

15 Volleyball

History

Volleyball celebrated its one hundredth anniversary in 1995. Originally the game was called 'mignonette', and was a recreational game for middle aged men. The purpose of the game was to hit the ball (a basketball bladder) over a tennis net with the hands.

In 1896 the game was renamed volleyball. Later, the net height was increased and teams were reduced to six players. The court was enlarged and a special lighter leather ball was produced for the game.

It became an Olympic Sport in 1964. Today there are over 150 million people playing the game. The International Volleyball Federation is one of the largest and fastest growing sports bodies, and is the second largest participant sport in the world after soccer.

'Volley' is a term used in any sport where the ball is played before it hits the ground. This therefore is the main purpose of the game, to keep the ball in play before it hits the ground. Other sports where the volley is always used are badminton, and sepaktapraw, which is played in Indonesia, Malaysia, the Philippines, and in the Northern Territory of Australia. Other sports which use volleying from time to time are tennis, squash, soccer, and cricket.

Volleyball was introduced into Papua New Guinea schools in the 1950's. In 1973 the first National Championships were organised with teams attending from EHP, Lae, Finschhafen and Port Moresby. The National Championships have now become an annual event, with more teams participating from different parts of the country. In 1975, Papua New Guinea sent its first volleyball group to compete in the Fifth South Pacific Games in Guam. A men's team and a women's team attended, gaining valuable experience in playing in an international event.

Some of the best world teams today include:

Men's: Italy, Cuba, Brazil, Japan, USA, Netherlands

Women's: Cuba, Brazil, China

How to play

Each team has six players on the court, but may have up to six substitutes. In mini-volley for younger children, there are a maximum of six players, with four allowed on the court. Play is started by one player hitting the ball by hand over the net. This server can stand anywhere behind the base line. There is no longer a service box area, from which to serve.

Once the ball passes over the net the receiving team is allowed to touch the ball three times before it must go back over the net. No player, however, may hit the ball twice in succession. The purpose of the game is to hit the ball to the ground inside the opposition's half of the court, or to force them into making errors so that they are unable to return the ball. The ball may be played back on either the first, second or third touch. Modern tactics, however, aim to use all three touches to build up a strong attack.

Figure 15.1 Volleyball is a popular game in most schools

The normal pattern is as follows:

- the first touch gets the ball close to the net; this skill is called a bump, or dig
- the second touch is to play it high above and close to the net; this skill is called a volley, or set
- the final touch is a hard, one handed hit over the net; this skill is called a spike, or smash.

The opposing team tries to intercept the smash by using one, two or even three players jumping up together to form a wall with their hands. This is called a block. If the serving team wins the rally it scores a point, but if the receiving team wins, it gains the right to serve.

Scoring

A set is won by the team that first scores 15 points with a minimum lead of two points. In the case of a 14–14 tie, the play is continued until a two-point lead is reached, e.g. 16–14, 17–15. However, in the first four sets, a point limit is reached at 17. After a 16–16 tie, the team scoring the 17th point wins the set with only a one-point lead. In the deciding set, in the case of a 14–14 tie, play is continued until a 2-point lead is reached. There is no point limit. A match is won by the team that wins three sets.

In the case of a 2–2 tie, the deciding fifth set is played as a tie-break, with the 'rally point' scoring system. This is where a point is scored whenever a team wins a rally, whether the team has served or not. In any sport where a ball is struck over a net (such as tennis or volleyball), a 'rally' is where the ball is played by both teams over the net several times before one player or team is unable to get it back correctly.

Figure 15.2 The skills of volleyball can be practised on any flat surface

The court

This can be a mini-volley court size of 12 m long and 6 m wide, to the full size court of 18 m long and 9 m wide. An attack line is marked 3 m from the net.

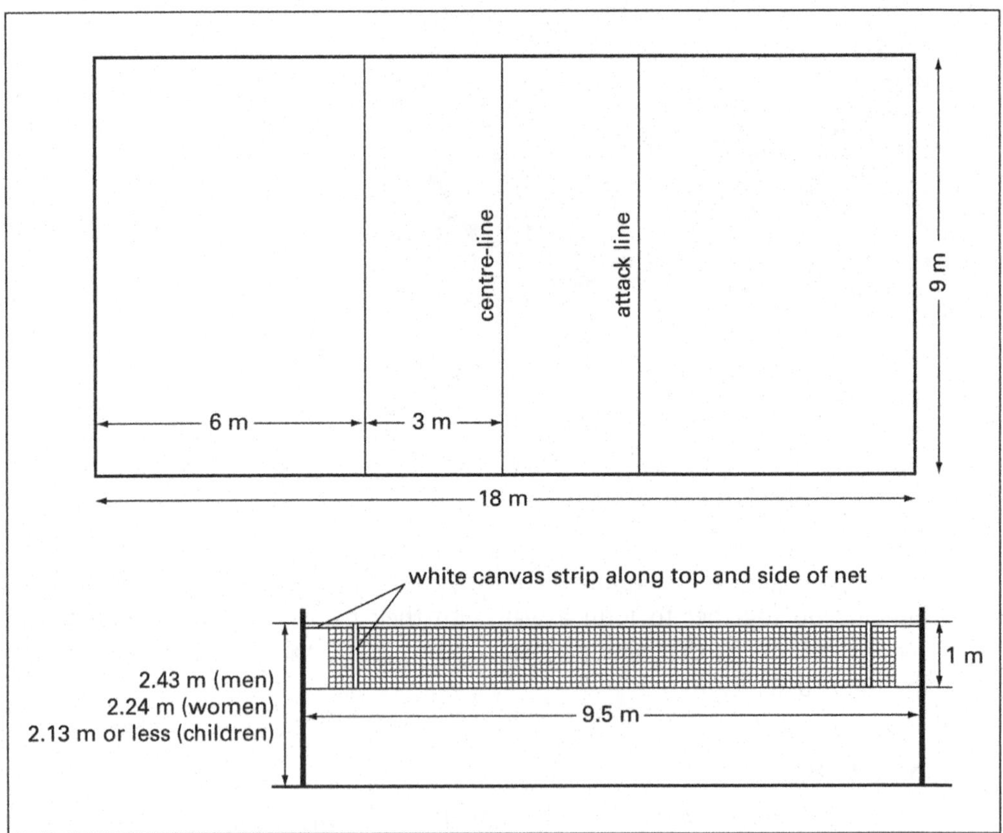

Figure 15.3 Volleyball court markings and dimensions

Equipment

Volleyball does not require expensive equipment, and can be played on almost any flat area.

Figure 15.4 How high do you think this net is?

Net

The net is suspended tightly across the centre of the court and should be at a height of 2 m for mini-volley, 2.24 m for women, and 2.43 m for men.

Figure 15.5 Knee-pads are optional

Ball

A size four or five mini-volleyball, or a standard volleyball may be used. The ball should not be fully inflated like a soccer or basketball. Foam balls can be used by younger players just starting to play the game.

Footwear

This should be light-weight and non-slip for playing inside. Knee-pads are optional.

Some volleyball terms

Attack lines

The lines parallel with and drawn 3 m from the centre line. This is the area from which no back court player may smash.

Beach volleyball

A popular version of volleyball played, with two persons per team, on beach sand. It became an Olympic sport for the first time in Atlanta in 1996.

Block

One, two, or three front line players attempt to intercept the ball near and above the net by forming a wall of hands.

Figure 15.6 Practising the dig

Carry

Contacting the ball longer than allowed by the rules.

Contact

A ball which touches or is touched by any part of a player's body or his/her clothing.

Dig

A technique of playing the ball on the forearms, usually below waist level.

Double foul
Fouls committed at the same moment by opposing players.

Dink
A technique used to tap the ball lightly over the hands of the opponent's block.

Etiquette
When returning the ball to the other end of the court, roll it back along the floor. Each team should line up on the baseline at the commencement and completion of the set.

Held ball
The ball is delayed in the hands or arms when being played.

Match
The best of three or five sets, depending on the competition. All international matches are the best of five sets.

Mini-volley
A game of volleyball played between teams of fewer than the normal six players, usually three or four per side.

Figure 15.7 Did the player touch the net?

Net fault
A player touches the net when the ball is in play.

Pass
The controlled moving of the ball from one player to another on the same team.

Point
When the serving team wins the rally and the team's score is increased by one.

Quick smash
A smash performed before the opponents can counter with a block.

Rally
A stage in the game from when the ball is served until it is 'dead'.

Referee
The match official in charge of the game. The referee uses a whistle and hand signals to control the game.

Rotation
Each member of the new serving side must move around one position in a clockwise direction, before play can be recommenced.

Service
Putting the ball into play.

Figure 15.8 Setting the ball

Service area
The area behind the base line.

Set
A game to a minimum of fifteen points with a two point lead. If there is not a two point lead, the game continues until this is the case.

Setter
The player at the net who distributes passes to his smashers.

Side out
The non-serving team wins the rally, and receives the right to serve. No points are scored on a side out.

Smash or spike
The technique of hitting the ball downwards and hard into the opponent's court from above the level of the net.

Substitution
When the ball is 'dead' a player on court may be replaced by a team substitute.

Time out
A period of thirty seconds for a brief rest and coaching. Each team is allowed two time-outs per set.

Volley
The most accurate pass in the game, played by using both hands. The ball is usually passed in the direction the player is facing, with the ball played on the fingertips in front of and just above the forehead.

Figure 15.9 Practising a volley

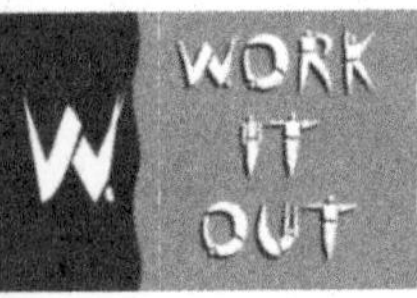

WORK IT OUT!

Answer the following questions and write your answers in your exercise book. The answers to these questions will be found on page 156 at the back of the book.

1. What was the original name of the game of volleyball?
2. In what year did volleyball become an Olympic sport?
3. What is the only world sport with more participants than volleyball?
4. How many players are there in a volleyball team?
5. Where must the server stand to serve?
6. How many times can the ball be contacted before it must go over the net?
7. Name the final skill where the ball is hit hard over the net with one hand.
8. What is the minimum points lead a team must have to win a set?
9. When may a team make player substitutions?
10. How many 'time-outs' may a team have in one set?

Unscramble the Words

Unscramble the following letters to find words about volleyball.

1. yeabvlloll
2. klboc
3. keips
4. tisttbsoinuu
5. yrall
6. rcetetpni
7. ptecioner
8. pbmu
9. eeeerrf
10. aetm

16 Cricket

History

It is not possible to say exactly where or when the game of cricket started, however it was being played as long ago as, the sixteenth century in England. The British had considered sport as a way to build character in youth, and in the late nineteenth century when the London Missionary Society settled in the South Pacific islands, they brought cricket with them.

In Noumea and the nearby islands, teams play for an annual cup on the anniversary of French occupation. Runs, known as 'pines', are scored by running up and down the pitch until the ball is returned to the wicket-keeper, because there are no boundaries.

In early cricket played in Fiji, the tribal chief has the divine right to always bat first, and then not to take any further part in the game.

In other Pacific islands the local version of the game became the place to carry out a battle, rather than use bows and arrows. Each village batted and fielded in turn. At the end of the game the losers provided the food for the feast.

Cricket was first introduced to the Trobriand Islands in Milne Bay Province, Papua New Guinea. The Trobriand Islanders introduced their own rules to the game, and even today Trobriand cricket is quite different from cricket played anywhere else. Trobriand cricket is played during yam festivals to celebrate the harvest, and competition and rivalry are less important than the celebration. The game is accompanied by a lot of singing and dancing. As a custom, the visitors usually lose the game to show respect to their hosts. Importantly, they use traditional skills to produce appropriate equipment out of locally available materials to suit their needs and their culture.

Cricket has been played in Papua New Guinea for many decades, and has been included in the school curriculum. There are very popular cricket competitions in several provinces, however, not many schools have tried to teach it in Physical Education classes. Papua New Guinea has a very successful team in the South Pacific region, has participated in some international competitions, and has performed very well, getting into semi-finals against other nations in recent years. The national team competed in the Commonwealth Games tournament in Malaysia in 1998. If both primary and secondary schools include cricket as part of both boys' and girls' sport activities, there is potential for the development of high quality skills and success at all levels across the country.

Starting cricket

Cricket can be played simply in schools, with very little cost. It is only necessary to buy expensive equipment at the highest level of cricket.

To start learning cricket you can use a tennis ball and a simple wooden bat. The stumps can be made from three pieces of straight wood or thin branches. The main skills of bowling, batting, fielding (catching and throwing), and keeping wicket can be learned through lots of practice. The more you practise, the more skilful you will become. In time, equipment may be purchased to play the full adult version of the game. But even at secondary school the game is very enjoyable using simple equipment. Students should have three or four years experience playing with the soft ball, such as a tennis ball, before moving on to use the hard ball. The main purpose of the game is for the team to score more runs in total than the opposing team. If the number of runs is the same, then the team having fewer batters 'out' wins.

The playing field

Cricket is played on a hard smooth surface called a pitch, that is 20.5 m long. This is set in the middle of a large grassed area. In dry areas the pitch may be without grass as long as it is smooth and without bumps, stones, sticks, or anything else that could hurt a player if s/he fell. The ball must bounce evenly on the pitch. The edge of the ground is usually marked out so that a ball hit past this boundary scores extra runs.

Wickets, made up of sets of three sticks set in the ground 20.5 m distance from each other act as targets for a bowler. The bowler has six attempts (in an set of bowls called an *over*) to get the batter out. The batter stands in front of the wicket (also called the *stumps* because they are like small, narrow tree stumps) and tries to stop the ball from hitting them. The batter defends by stopping the ball hitting the stumps.

The batter (or striker) tries to score as many runs as possible. This is done by hitting the bowled ball away from the fielders, and s/he and the other batter (called the non-striker) run between the two wickets, changing places, to the safe area at the other end, called the *crease*. (The crease is shown by a straight line marked on the ground at either end of the pitch.

The players

There are eleven players per team. Each team must bat, two players at a time, and when ten players are 'out' then the other team must bat. As each batter is 'out', that player's place is taken by the next person, until the ten players are out.

Each team has a specialist wicket-keeper, as well as several players who bowl well. However, everyone must bat at some time in their team's innings.

The number of bowlers depends upon the rules of the competition that is being played. In school cricket, the maximum number of overs that a bowler might bowl could be limited to five, or perhaps ten overs. In international test cricket, they are unlimited.

The types of bowling varies. Some bowlers bowl very fast, while others slow down so that the ball swings, or changes direction through the air. Others make the ball change direction a little when it hits the pitch. Some are *cutters* (the seam or stitching on the ball hits the ground at an angle, and it changes direction by a few important centimetres) and others are *spinners* (the bowler uses fingers or the wrist to make the ball spin as it is bowled, and it changes direction to trick the striker).

Rules

According to the type of competition, the game will last so that each team receives about the same number of bowls, or overs. This depends on the time available, for example, half a day, or a whole day, or even just half an hour per team. Test matches between two countries may last up to five days.

The same bowler bowls an *over* (six bowls) from one end. Then another bowler bowls an over from the other end. The captain selects another bowler if the bowler is tiring, or the team is not getting the batters out. The batters change ends according to how many runs they can score from a hit. There are several ways of getting a batter out. These include:

- the bowled ball hits the striker's wicket
- the ball is caught by a fielder from the striker's hit
- the ball hits the striker's leg (and not the bat) in front of the wicket, and the umpire believes that the ball would have hit the wicket (balled 'Leg Before Wicket' or LBW)
- the wicket-keeper stumps the striker (catching the ball and using it to hit the stumps) when the striker has moved out of the safe crease area
- the batter does not reach the safety of the crease before the ball is returned by a fielder to hit the wickets

Skills

There are six main skills areas that are required in cricket. Not everyone on the team will perform all of them, but when first learning, everyone should try each skill.

1. Batting

Everyone must bat at some time. Some, however, will become specialist batters because of their eyesight, timing, and coordination. Some will be good attackers, and others good defenders. When learning to bat, use a tennis or a rubber ball. Any sort of bat can be used, but an old one, or one that is not too heavy and not too big, should be used.

Right handers will have the right hand low on the grip, and the left hand towards the top of the bat handle. Stand sideways towards the bowler, with feet slightly apart.

Figure 16.1 Holding the bat correctly

Watch the bowler run up to the wicket to bowl. As the bowler's arm comes over the top to bowl, lift the bat off the ground, ready to swing it towards the approaching ball. This is very important if the bowler is fast as you need time to hit safely. If your hands are in front of the bottom of the bat, the ball will stay down when you hit it. If the front (or face) of the bat is up, then the ball will go up, giving the chance of a catch.

To *defend forwards*, when the ball is landing close to you, step towards the ball, pushing your hands forward so that the ball hits the bat, goes to the ground, and cannot be caught. Do not swing the bat, and keep it straight.

Figure 16.2 Defending forwards

To *attack forwards*, if the ball is bouncing close to you, step towards it, swing the bat hard through the line of the ball and follow the swing through over your shoulder. Keep the bat straight, and grip it tightly.

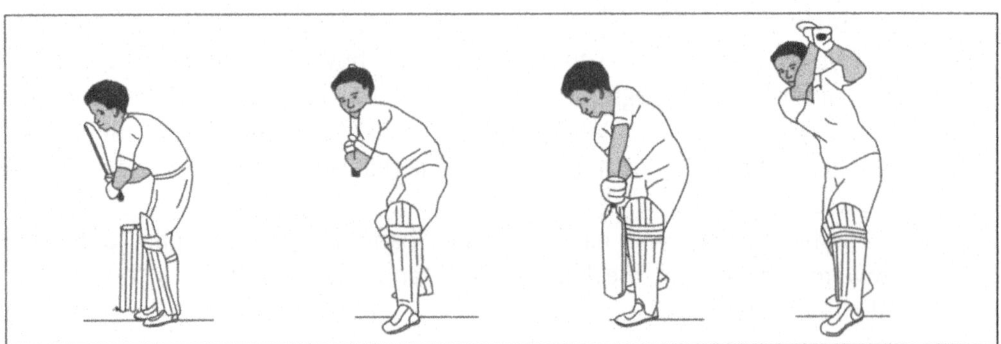

Figure 16.3 Attacking forwards

HAVE A GO!

Practise the two *forward* shots by hitting the ball off a low height (5 cm–10 cm) on the ground, e.g.

- from a small pile of soil
- from a small box or ice-cream container
- from a tuft of grass

With the defensive shot, the ball will hardly move forwards at all.
With the attacking shot the ball should travel as far as your strength can make it. To ensure maximum success, watch the ball as long as possible onto the bat. Your head needs to keep as still as possible.

2. Bowling

Everyone should be able to bowl in some way. Most bowls are aimed at the stumps, trying to cause the striker to make a mistake. The ball hitting the pitch just in front of the striker can make the ball change direction and so deceive the striker. This causes the striker to miss the ball so that it hits the stumps, or cause the striker to be out LBW. Or the striker hits the ball into the air and is caught out. The fast bowler, usually the first to use the new ball, can beat the striker simply by being very fast.

HAVE A GO!

Try the following activity in groups, taking it in turns to practise batting, bowling and fielding. When first learning to bowl, the distance from the target can be just a few metres away. As you get better, increase the distance to the full length of the pitch.

1. Stand sideways with the ball in the fingers of the hand away from the target.
2. Lean sideways slightly, towards the ball side, with feet apart. Keep your head up.
3. Keep looking sideways over your shoulder at the target. This is usually the bottom or base of the stumps.
4. With the ball in your fingers and your arm straight (you are not allowed to bend, jerk or change the angle at your elbow—this is a throw), reach back. Then as you step towards the striker, swing your arm high over your shoulder to bowl the ball as straight as possible to your target.
5. Your body weight starts from the back foot, then moves over to the front foot as you bowl the ball.
6. The front foot should be nearly pointing down the pitch at the striker.
7. Let your arm and body move through naturally after you let the ball go.
8. Try a three, then five step slow run-up approach. Make sure your foot nearest the striker has some part of the foot behind the crease line. If not, it is called 'No Ball', the batter cannot be caught out, bowled or LBW, and an extra run is scored.

To help you bowl more accurately, try the following with a partner:

1. Place a hoop or other target on the pitch just in front of the stumps, where you think the bowled ball should land in order to hit the stumps.
2. Practise bowling the ball to land in the hoop, or as near as possible. In turns, practise bowling into the hoop. See who can score the most?

3. Your partner can be the wicket-keeper, standing just behind and to the right (called 'off' in cricket) side of the stumps. Can you hit just the off stump?

4. Try a combination game of six bowls each, with the following scores:

- land the ball in the hoop — 3 points
- hit the stumps — 2 points
- land the ball in the hoop and hits the stumps — 10 points

3. Fielding

Everyone must learn how to field. Some players are good throwers, and are able to field long hits or catch big hits towards the boundary. Even though the ball may not come to them often, they must always be ready to be in the correct position (chosen by the captain), and to run to the ball, pick it up quickly (without fumbling) and throw it back immediately and accurately.

Some fielders are placed close to the pitch, ready for quick catches or, if the batter moves out of the crease for a moment, to take the chance to throw the ball at the stumps to run the batter out. The different fielding positions are shown on Figure 16.4.

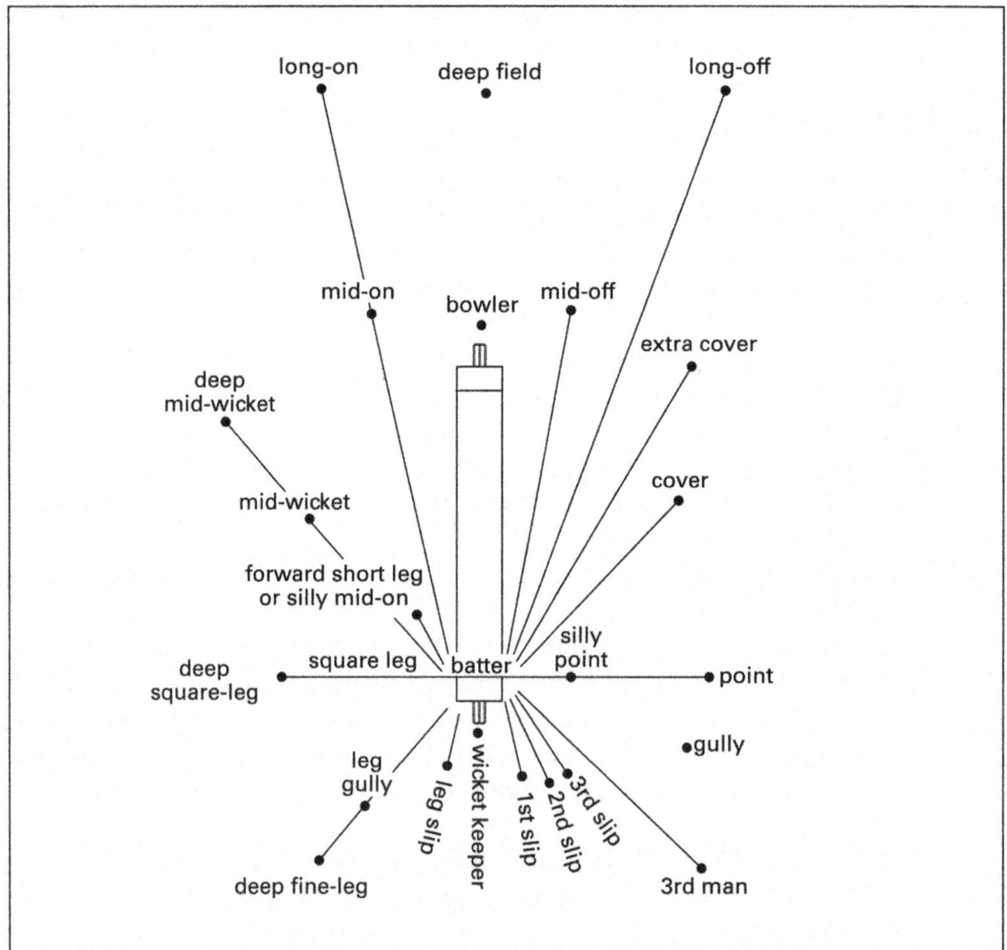

Figure 16.4 The fielding positions

Even if a ball is going straight to one fielder, it is important that another fielder is running around to support or back up the fielder, in case it is missed and gets past. This is also very important if a fielder throws the ball at the stumps for a run-out attempt, and misses.

4. Catching

Catching requires lots of practice. Other than the wicket-keeper, everyone uses bare hands, and so catching requires good eyesight, timing, and coordination to make sure the ball is not dropped. A batter who has scored just a few runs when a catch is dropped may go on to make many more runs to win the match.

When you see the ball coming in your direction, keep watching it into your hands. Point you fingers up or down, depending if it is a high or a low flighted ball. As the ball arrives at your hands, let the fingers wrap around the ball, and let your hands move or 'give'. A stiff handed catch will most often see the ball bounce out and be dropped. And your hand hurts!

5. Throwing

Good fielding must be supported by good throwing. This means knowing how hard and how straight to throw the ball in different situations, especially if there is the chance to have the batter out of the crease. It is very important in cricket to stop the batters scoring too many runs. This can be done with fast, accurate fielding and throwing back to the wicket-keeper or the bowler.

6. Keeping wicket

Each team has one specialist wicket-keeper. This is a difficult and tiring responsibility because the keeper has no opportunity to rest. This person must be ready to stop every ball bowled by the bowler. Additional runs are scored (called byes) for every ball that the wicket-keeper lets past.

In a game the keeper must wear pads to protect the legs, boots to protect the toes, and heavy leather, rubber gloves. Boys and men must also wear a 'box', which protects their groin.

Figure 16.5 The wicket keeper standing ready for the catch

17 Hockey

History

Early in the twentieth century, drawings of six different sporting activities were found in tombs in the Nile Valley in Egypt. One of these drawings shows two men holding what look like hockey sticks. The tomb was built around 2050 BC, over 4000 years ago. There are other examples of games similar to hockey. The Romans played a stick and ball game called paganica. The Irish still play a very old game called hurling, while the Scots play shinty, and the Welsh play bandy. The French game called hoquet was similar to hockey.

The name 'hockey' dates back to 1527, when it was spelt hockie. The modern day game of hockey is attributed to the English. Games were played between unlimited numbers of energetic boys and men (women did not take part in those early years).

The rules first appeared in 1868 at Eton College. Teams were restricted to eleven players per side, a goal scoring area, and a 'bully-off' to start the game. The first hockey association was formed in 1875. Since this time, hockey has become an international sport, and in 1908 it was first played at the Olympic Games. The Federation of International Hockey was formed with 47 countries as members.

There are now three types of hockey found in sports competitions around the world. The main type is sometimes called 'field hockey' because it is played outdoors on a grassed, or synthetic grass, field or pitch. The main playing nations of field hockey are Australia, Germany, Great Britain, India, the Netherlands, Pakistan, South Korea, and Spain.

Ice hockey is very popular in cold countries with lots of snow and ice. This is played as a sport on large ice rinks (like frozen lakes) in countries such as the U.S.A., Canada, Russia, Finland, and Sweden. Instead of a ball, a small flat rubber disk called a puck is used to push and hit across the ice.

Hockey can also be played indoors in large stadiums such as the Sir John Guise Stadium in Port Moresby. This is a very fast game because the ball may be bounced off the walls. It is better to play inside when the sun is too hot, or when it is raining outside.

Hockey is still quite new to Papua New Guinea. However, as Physical Education teachers are learning the sport, so the game will reach out more and more throughout the country. Television programmes showing hockey being played at the international level, such as in the World Cup and the Olympics, may also make young people interested in trying it for the first time.

The aim of the game

Hockey is played between two opposing teams of eleven players. The aim of the game is to shoot a hard ball into the opposing team's goal mouth, using a curved stick to hit the ball. The team that scores the most goals wins the game. The first time you watch a game of hockey you might think it looks difficult and dangerous. After all, any game where you may get a crack on the shins with a lump of wood can put you off! By learning the skills of the game, the rules, and by wearing proper equipment, hockey becomes a 'thinking' game, as well as a running game. In this way, you learn the essentials of playing in a team as well as using individual skills.

Many mini-games can be played. Young children can start with the game of *minkey* using tennis balls or soft rubber balls. Minkey has six players per side. It can be played on a netball size court or in one third of a full hockey field. Junior players can then advance to half-field hockey where there are seven players per side. The extra player is the goalkeeper.

Success in hockey depends upon skill, and not on physical aggression. Because of this, hockey can be easily taught to a mixed group of students.

The playing field

The playing ground needs to be reasonably level and smooth, without bumps or hollows, and it must be cleared of stones and sticks. If it is grass, then the grass should be smooth and without clumps or tufts of grass. The playing ground could also be a sand surface, or firm soil, that covers a firm base. The ball must be able to roll quickly and straight, without bouncing unevenly.

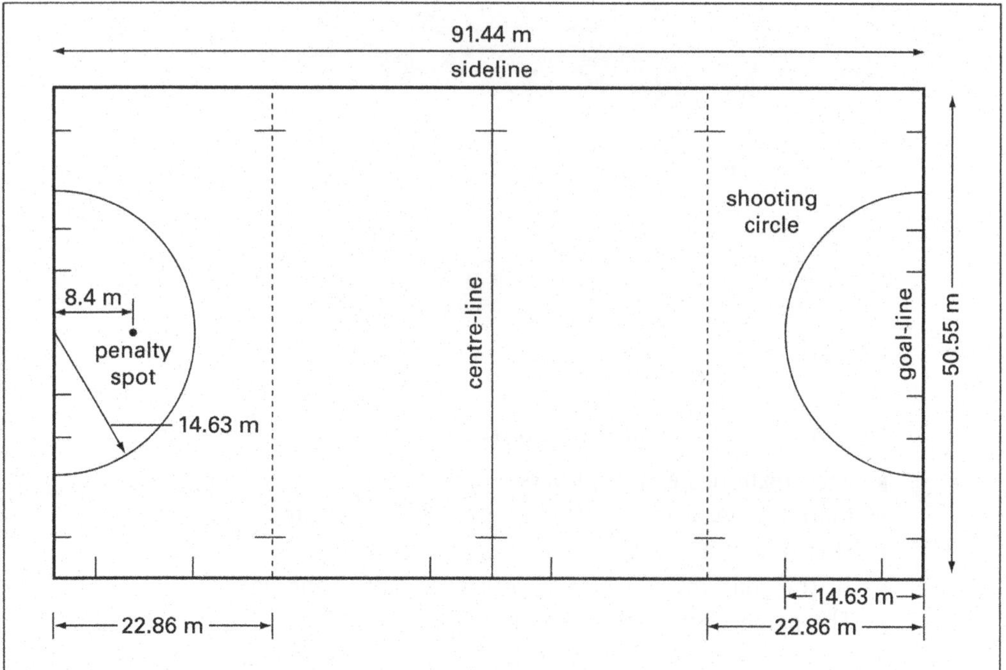

Figure 17.1 Dimensions of the hockey field

At either end of the field are the hockey goals. The hockey goals must have firm nets. There is a backboard and sideboard at the bottom which must be hit for a goal to be scored from a short corner, otherwise the goal does not count. In normal play, a goal is scored as long as the ball crosses the line.

Equipment

- a hockey stick
- running shoes or boots, with socks
- shin guards or pads
- mouth guard
- shirt, shorts, or skirt
- a hockey ball

Figure 17.2 Practising before the start of the game

How to play the game

- Each team has eleven players.
- Matches are made up of two halves of 35 minutes each.
- Half time lasts for 5–10 minutes.
- At the start you must be in your own half of the field.
- The game starts with a pass back.
- To score a goal you must shoot from within the goal circle, and the ball must pass completely across the goal line.

- The team that scores the goal does not get the next push back.
- The team is made up of attackers and defenders (very much the same as for soccer). The positions are worked out based on which side of the field you play on, e.g. left, right, or in the centre; and which role you play in the team, e.g. defender (full-back, half-back), midfielder, or striker.
- There are no restrictions as to where a player can play.
- There is no offside. (This rule was removed after the 1996 Olympics.)

Some of the rules of hockey

1. Only the face or flat side of the stick may be used for playing the ball.
2. The stick must be held in the hand by the player, including the goalkeeper, when making any play.
3. When playing or approaching the ball, the player may not raise any part of the stick above shoulder level.
4. The ball may not be undercut, nor may it be played in a dangerous way, or in a way likely to lead to dangerous play.
5. A ball may not be kicked, thrown, carried or pushed in any manner, except by the stick.
6. A player may not hit, hook, hold, strike at, or interfere with an opponent's stick.
7. A player may not charge, kick, shove, trip, strike at, or handle an opponent or opponent's clothing.
8. A player shall not obstruct an opponent by running between that player and the ball, or place the stick in a way which prevents an opponent from playing or approaching the ball.
9. A player shall not use the foot or leg to support the stick.
10. A player may tackle from the left of an opponent provided that the ball is played without previous interference with the stick or body of the opponent.
11. The goalkeeper may kick or stop the ball with any part of the body, but only when the ball is inside the circle.

Skills of the game

The skills will be shown to you by your teacher in practical sessions. The main ones are as follows.

Gripping the stick

As any movement of the ball must be done with the stick, it is important to have an understanding of an efficient grip. The left hand is always at the top of the stick and the right some 30 cm down the handle. The position of the right hand will vary according to the skill being performed. For example, when hitting the ball, the hands are together, when pushing the ball, the hands are further apart. It is important to remember that there are no left-handed hockey sticks. All sticks are the same shape, and can be used by people who are either left or right-handed. Sticks simply vary in length, according to how tall or short you are.

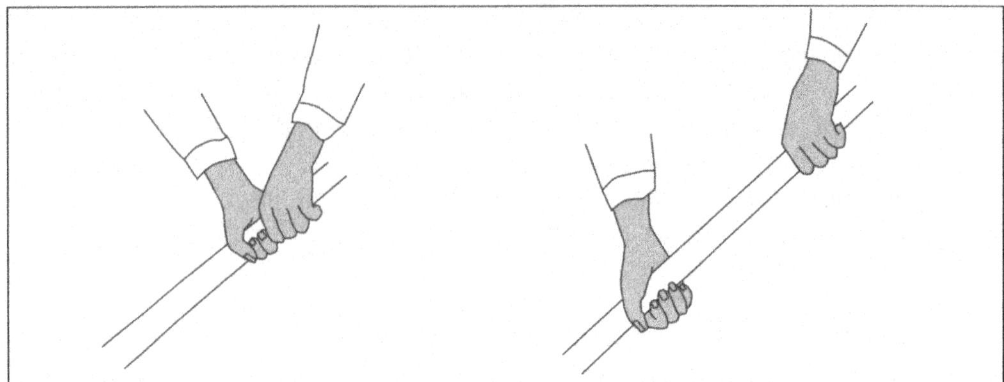

Figure 17.3 Gripping the stick

Figure 17.4 Trapping the ball

Receiving or trapping the ball

This is a skill in which the ball is controlled by trapping it on your stick, moving it into position, and setting it up for a pass. Remember, the ball can not touch your feet and you can only use the flat side of the stick.

Figure 17.5 Pushing the ball

Passing the ball

The most important aspect of the pass is to ensure accuracy and timing. Hockey is a team game and so passing is very important. The most commonly used pass is the push; it is the stroke to use whenever you are passing the ball over a short distance. It can be done quickly and it is easy to disguise.

Hitting the ball

When it is important that the ball travels at high speed, then it is hit firmly and hard. It is an important skill to clear the ball out of defence or to shoot at goal.

Figure 17.6 Hitting the ball

Lifting the ball

The final type of passing is when the ball is lifted. If there is space behind your opponents, you may lift the ball over them to land in that space, when you are trying to clear the ball. The techniques used are the scoop and the flick.

Figure 17.7 Getting ready to scoop the ball

Dribbling

This is the skill of moving the ball along the ground with your stick. You can work around your opponent and carry the ball along with you to advance in the field. There are five types of dribbling: open, closed, indian, reverse, and two handed reverse. The kind of dribble used will vary according to the situation. In all dribbling the dexterity (speed, flexibility, and strength) of the hands is vital as this determines how the ball is controlled and directed.

Figure 17.8 Different ways of dribbling

Tackling

This is where you can challenge an opponent for the ball. You must position yourself and the ball correctly if you are to gain possession. The different types of tackles are the poke, the block, and the lunge.

Goalkeeping

Goalkeepers require additional qualities, which can be developed by training. These are confidence, judgement, agility and mobility, quick reflexes. The goalkeeper uses the whole body to stop, block, or deflect the ball away from the goal. The goalkeeper must wear protective clothing and equipment such as; a helmet, a pair of padded gloves, a chest protector, suitable shoes/boots, special padded pants and vests. S/he is also expected to organise the other defensive players within the goal circle area. The goalie is allowed to raise the stick above the shoulder, and use hands and feet to stop the ball.

HAVE A GO!

In your groups, practise the skills of hockey described in the chapter. Remember, the more you practise, the better you will play the game.

WORK IT OUT!

Answer the following questions, and write the answers in your exercise book. You will find the correct answers on page 156, at the back of this book.

1. When was the first hockey association formed?
2. How many players are allowed on the field for one team?
3. How is a game of hockey started?
4. Is there an offside rule in hockey?
5. What is the only side of the stick which may be used?
6. Name three defensive positions.
7. What is the most commonly used passing skill or technique?
8. What is the name of the skill in which the ball is moved along the ground?
9. Name some special skills required by the goal keeper.

10. Which hand is at the top of the stick?

11. Copy the following word puzzle into your exercise book, and circle the hockey terms in the word puzzle.

DRIBBLE, GOALIE, STICK, BACK, PUSH, HOCKEY, FREE HIT, MOVE, HIT, DODGE, PASS, OFFSIDE, FLICK, SPEED, TACKLE, SCOOP, BALL, CORNER, SKILL, GRIP, PENALTY, FORWARD, TRAP, INNER, VISION, WING

E	I	L	A	O	G	Y	P	I	R	G
V	I	S	I	O	N	T	K	D	S	I
L	E	L	I	S	K	L	R	E	O	D
R	B	G	A	C	C	A	E	E	L	R
T	E	F	D	O	A	N	N	P	K	A
I	A	N	C	O	B	E	R	S	T	W
H	G	H	N	P	D	P	O	A	Y	R
E	N	O	C	I	H	E	C	O	H	O
E	I	K	S	O	E	K	C	I	L	F
R	W	F	C	E	L	C	K	O	L	T
F	F	K	V	E	B	L	I	G	I	R
O	E	O	E	C	B	S	L	T	K	A
Y	M	E	P	A	I	R	T	A	S	P
S	S	A	P	V	R	S	I	W	B	A
S	T	I	C	K	D	C	H	S	U	P

Answers

Chapter 2 Your Body

Page 16

1. 206 2. knee, ankle, wrist, shoulder, hip 3. knee 4. a. pectorals b. deltoids c. abdominals d. quadriceps e. biceps

Page 19

1. atria (or atriums), ventricles 2. a. (iv) b. (i) c. (v) d. (vi) e. (ii) f. (iii)

Page 22

2. a. incisors b. molars c. is broken down 3. a. T b. F c. F d. T e. F f. T g. T h. T i. T j. T

Chapter 9 Swimming

Page 90

1. 1896 2. Side-stroke, breast-stroke 3. Healy 4. Australia 5. Butterfly 6. Survival back-stroke or side-stroke 7. to conserve energy 8. stay relaxed 9. fat person 10. higher

Chapter 10 Softball

Page 99

1. After being hit by a pitched ball while batting. When the pitcher pitches four 'balls'. 2. To advance a baserunner 3. True 4. T bol 5. American World War II soldiers 6. Infield 7. Right Outfield 8. Plate Umpire 9. Designated Batter 10. Home Run.
11. Leaving a base before the ball has left the pitcher's hand, **or** when a baserunner is tagged running between bases, **or** when a baserunner runs on a fly ball that is successfully caught and doesn't return to touch the previous base, **or** when a forced out is made, **or** when the baserunner swerves outside the 0.9 m line when running from base to base, **or** when the baserunner interferes with a fielder attempting to field the ball. 12. False

Chapter 15 Volleyball

Page 140

1. 'Mignonette' 2. 1964 3. Soccer 4. 12 5. Anywhere along the base line 6. 3 7. Spike or smash 8. 2 points 9. At any time when the ball is 'dead' 10. 2

Answers to word scramble

1. volleyball 2. block 3. spike 4. substitution 5. rally 6. intercept 7. reception 8. bump 9. referee 10. team

Chapter 17 Hockey

Page 154

1. 1875 2. 11 3. A push back 4. No. (Not since the Olympic Games in 1996.) 5. Flat 6. Full back, half back, goal keeper 7. Push 8. Dribbling 9. Confidence, judgement, agility and mobility, quick reflexes 10. Left

Useful addresses

Youth Sports Coordinator
Papua New Guinea Sports Commission
P.O. Box 1991
Boroko
NCD 111
Papua New Guinea

Curriculum Officer, Physical Education
Curriculum Development Division
Department of Education
P.O. Box 446
Waigani
NCD 131
Papua New Guinea

Director
National Sports Institute
P.O. Box 337
Goroka
Eastern Highlands Province 441
Papua New Guinea

Printed in Australia
08 Feb 2019
698341

9 780195 541236